THE
24-HOUR
TURN-AROUND

THE
24-HOUR
TURN-AROUND

Change Your Life One Hour at a Time

Jim Hartness and Neil Eskelin

SPIRE

© 1993 by Jim Hartness and Neil Eskelin

Published by Revell
a division of Baker Publishing Group
P.O. Box 6287, Grand Rapids, Michigan 49516-6287
www.revellbooks.com

Mass Market edition published 2017

ISBN 978-0-8007-2869-4

Printed in the United States of America

17   18   19   20   21   22   23   7   6   5   4   3   2   1

Contents

Contents

your greatest decision

Can a positive—and permanent—transformation take place in the time it takes the earth to circle the sun? Is it possible that your life can be dramatically changed in just one day?

It is not only possible, but *probable*.

This book is based on a very simple premise. The great changes that affect your life are not made progressively over long periods of time. They are the result of conscious decisions that you make at specific moments. These are not hasty choices but are deeply rooted resolutions resulting in significant changes of your thoughts and actions.

For example, you may take six months to reach your diet goal of losing twenty pounds. But you won the battle much earlier—at the precise hour you made a total commitment. The same process applies to all of the changes we seek in our lives.

When will the transformation begin? The moment you decide to change. Changes will take place one hour at a time as you come face-to-face with challenges that may be the greatest you have ever chosen to confront. In this book you are being asked to make an intense and personal commitment.

This volume was not designed to be read in a specific period of time. What we ask is that you spend one hour totally focused on each individual chapter. Read it, think about it, and make the deep, heartfelt decision that is necessary for change.

Here is what you'll discover. By making a total commitment in several important domains, the decisions become linked and layered, resulting in strength and power you never dreamed possible. This will affect your work life, your physical body, your personal relationships, and your overall attitude.

Where does it begin? Ask any psychologist, counselor, or therapist and you'll get one answer: *Nothing happens without a decision to change.*

As you continue reading, you'll be asked to make decisions regarding your thoughts, your goals, your attitudes, and your habits. But making decisions about specific changes will be a futile exercise without making the most important decision of all—deciding to be willing and open to change.

You may say, "I've tried so many times before, but nothing seems to happen."

That's what the mountain climber could have said after three failed attempts to reach the top of Mount Everest. Instead, he looked up at the summit and said, "You defeated me once. You defeated me twice. You defeated me three times. But mountain, I will someday conquer you, because you cannot get any bigger and I can."

Whether you know it or not, everything—including your own body—is in a constant state of change. When you climb the same mountain again, it will be a totally new experience. The ancient Greek philosopher Heraclitus said, "You can't step into the same river twice." The water constantly moves down the river and out to sea.

Think about the Grand Canyon, remembering that those colorful gorges are the result of the rushing water of the Colorado River. Its erosion continues to wash down the river to the Mojave Desert of California. The Grand Canyon is changing—one grain of sand at a time.

Change is not something to dread; it's a sign of life. If all the cells in your body weren't constantly replacing themselves, you would die. The dictionary defines *change* as "putting something in place of something else." It is the process of alteration and replacement.

What Needs Changing?

Nothing's permanent. Your personality, your emotions, and your perception are in constant flux. What is frightening, however, is that most change happens to most people without direction, forethought, or personal control. When we don't think about changing, we are often surprised and disappointed that things happen to us. We react to outside circumstances, rather than deciding how we will change ourselves.

A common way of reacting is to change jobs, mates, or friends. People seem to think that if only they have the perfect boss or spouse or house, everything will be okay. But most people never think of consciously changing themselves.

Just look around and you'll observe two groups of people: those who are changing and those who are resisting change, even defending against it. The latter group would do well to heed the words of Washington Irving who wrote, "I have found in traveling in a stagecoach, that it is often a comfort to shift one's position and be bruised in a new place."

Whatever happened to those employees who said, "I'll never use a computer"? They're either working in a dead-end job, or they decided to join the data processing revolution. Successful people are "changing" people. They do what others are afraid of doing.

If corporations do not respond to consumer demands, they are headed for bankruptcy. How many times have you seen "new and improved" Ivory soap? What would you think if your doctor pulled out an antique scalpel instead of a high-tech laser instrument?

Do you recall the story Christ told of the old wineskins? They were inflexible, rigid, and dry—with no room for expansion. Many people are that way; they hold on to old ideas, unwilling to admit when they are wrong. Christ warned that we should not "put new wine into old wineskins, or else the wineskins break, and the wine is spilled, and the wineskins are ruined. But they put new wine into new wineskins, and both are preserved" (Matt. 9:17).

Change demands flexibility, elasticity, and a willingness to exchange old ideas for new ones.

What would be your reaction to the news that ten years from today your life would be exactly as it is right now? You probably wouldn't be thrilled with the prospect. That's why it is important to make a conscious decision to see your life transformed.

It's not something to delay. The process should begin immediately. An old proverb says, "We learn how to make decisions by making decisions."

As you begin, there are four vital things to know when making a commitment to change:

One. A decision, even if it is wrong, is a positive beginning and a sign of progress. The details of how to accomplish a task come after the decision to begin has been made. The decision itself releases the creativity and energy necessary to determine the strategy for the task ahead. Most people, however, never get past the decision-making phase. They want to know how to do it, may even make elaborate plans, but have not made the commitment. Indecision, if prolonged, results in a self-defeating cycle of doubt and fear. What is important about a mistake is what you discover from it. You can't learn from mistakes you don't make.

Jesus honored Peter's decision to walk on the water—knowing that he would sink. But he allowed Peter to fail because it was the key to learning and growth.

Two. Wrong decisions can be corrected, but a "zero" decision can't. We have the freedom to choose, which means we have the freedom to make complete fools of ourselves. We also have the freedom to *fail.* Only when we are free to fail are we free to examine, explore, and grow. If we want our horizons to expand, however, we should not choose to fail out of irresponsibility.

Three. Guidance comes only to things that are in motion. A parked car doesn't need direction; but once the motor is running and the wheels begin to turn, you can steer in the direction you want to travel. Once you've made a decision and have begun to implement it, you immediately feel the power that comes as you control and guide your plan.

Four. No one moves without a decision to move. If left to circumstances and outside influences, your life would lack direction. It would go on without purpose. That's why it is so dangerous to avoid making vital decisions for change. Trying to be fail-safe is a sure route to defeat.

Scientific progress comes from research. Hundreds and hundreds of failed experiments are necessary for just one tiny discovery. In view of progress, failure and research are synonymous.

Where Do You Begin?

Your initial question when looking at a road map is, "Where am I?" The first step in reaching a destination is to determine your present location.

People in the "helping" professions know that behavioral change will not occur until people discover where they are and begin to deal with what *is*. Most of the frustration people experience is based on failure to deal with present circumstances.

Scripture gives us a view from God's perspective. *He doesn't change us so that he can accept us. He accepts us so that he can change us.* And something else. Acceptance not only precedes change, but it is the *incentive* to change. Once we truly see things as they are, we somehow have more desire to be transformed.

An artist in his London studio looked down from his window at a homeless man who was curled up, lying in the street near the curb. The artist took out his sketchbook and began to draw the man. But what he drew became something totally different from what he saw. Gone was the wrinkled brow. No longer was the man curled up on the street. Instead, the artist showed him standing tall, with his shoulders squared.

The moment he finished the pencil drawing, the artist rushed down to the street and told the man, "Look, I've drawn your picture!"

The indigent couldn't believe what he was seeing. "Sir," he said as he rolled to one side, "is that how you see me?"

"Yes it is. Just like this picture." Then he said, "Here, you can have it."

The man rose to his feet and said, "If that's how you see me, that's the way I'm going to be."

Holding the picture in both his hands, standing straight and tall, he said, "Mister, I'm never going to return to this gutter again."

We are all products of the choices we make. And if we don't like the "product," we can be reshaped by our inherent ability to make new choices. So often people say, "If it were not for what has happened to me, things would be different." They begin to blame other people and external circumstances for their problems. As long as we see ourselves as victims, we will remain powerless to change.

Victims deny the cognitive faculty to direct their own lives. It's been said, "You can drown in six inches of mud if you lie down and wallow in it."

Albert Bandura, the founder of social cognitive theory, maintains that individuals have a decision in directing their own lives through what is called "reciprocal triadic determinism." In other words, three interrelated factors direct our lives. They are thoughts, actions, and surroundings.

External circumstances only *influence* our decisions. The final responsibility rests with internal dynamics. It is how we process information into thoughts that determines action. Knowledge *precedes* thought; it is what we think about that triggers our behavior.

First Things First

In the hours of this book that follow, you will be asked to make specific, long-term changes in highly focused areas of your life. Before that can happen, however, you must face a broader decision on which all other change depends. There comes a time when you must say, "Yes, I am willing to change!"

Right now, while concluding this chapter, find a place to get alone with your thoughts. It may be a private place in your home or in the solitude of a quiet walk. As you reflect on what you are being asked to do, take an inventory of where you are and where you want to be.

The shortest route from the starting point to your destination is the highway marked "Willingness to Change." Is it risky? Yes. Will there be failures? Definitely. Will people laugh at your intentions? Perhaps, unless you share them with those who are on your same level of personal growth. But remember, risk doesn't always lead to ruin, and failure isn't fatal. Detours won't matter if your compass is fixed on your new destination.

Albert Bandura tells us that our ability to visualize the final product becomes the powerful tool that enables us to process and transform our experiences into internal models and images that guide future actions. A total determination to change will employ virtually untapped capabilities that most people never utilize.

You won't have to be told when that moment of decision happens. You'll know it! You won't even need to speak the words, "I will." You'll feel them resonate from deep within. They will awaken your mind, your heart, and every fiber, from top to toe.

Are you ready for that kind of change?

The decision is yours.

revalue your self-worth

When we want an appraisal of our home, our jewelry, or any other valuable possession, we can look in the phone book for a professional to provide an opinion. But how can we determine what *we* are worth? Who sets the "price" on the value of an individual?

Most people write their own price tags and manage to grossly underestimate their value. Why? Because they concentrate on weakness rather than strength; on failure rather than success. Or, they compare themselves to others and say things like, "I don't have enough talent. I don't have the right education. I don't have enough money."

Few people are satisfied with themselves. They look at the bottom line of their assets and liabilities and enter a big zero. Poor self-perception is a source of emotional pain.

According to psychiatrist James P. Comer of Yale University, self-esteem is "the high and positive regard an individual has for the self."[1] But for many, the reality is that self-esteem is in the valley rather than on the mountain.

Ten Steps to a Transformed Self-Esteem

Here are some specific steps you can take that will lead to a profound difference in the way you perceive yourself.

Step One. Get acquainted with the real you. The legendary statement, "Know thyself," spoken by the Greek philosopher Socrates, is still a message for today.

Do you truly know yourself? Have you ever asked a friend, "Be honest; how do you see me? What are my strengths and my weaknesses?"

Dr. Jacob Needleman, professor of philosophy at San Francisco State University, says that modern psychology is primarily concerned with knowledge about oneself. Only you can come to a conscious inner awareness of who you really are.

If your problem is low self-esteem, there is no substitute for gaining insight into the problem. Research by psychologist Anne H. Baumgardner at Michigan State University shows a direct link between knowledge of oneself and self-esteem. In one study, students with low self-esteem, in an effort to boost their image, described themselves in a more positive, exaggerated manner than did those students possessing high self-esteem. But when asked to describe a close friend, those with low self-esteem provided less information, indicating doubts in their abilities to judge themselves and others.

Happiness, a manifestation of self-esteem, has often been described as "being at peace with oneself." It is vital that you have an honest and clear picture of what is happening on the inside. You have the ability to self-reflect and then attach value to the real you.

Step Two. Laugh at your handicaps. Have you ever met a "perfect" person? We haven't. There are flaws in everyone—including you.

What is important is that you don't allow handicaps to become permanent barriers.

Moses was "slow of speech," but it didn't hinder his ability to lead his people to the promised land.

Even Jesus had handicaps that could have provided an excuse for failure. He had an apparently scandalous birth, was born into a hated minority race, was called a "liar," a "heretic," and a "traitor to Caesar." But he knew something that more than compensated for any perceived weakness—he knew he was the Son of God.

Step Three. Put your failures in perspective. We all fail as children— falling hundreds of times before learning to walk and making thousands of mistakes on the road to becoming adults. But if we aren't careful, our responses to failure can result in lifelong negative patterns. They can lead to an avoidance of reality, low expectations, and perpetual disappointments.

A baseball star fails to hit the ball seven times out of ten, yet he is paid millions of dollars and called a hero. This is just one example of failure in perspective.

Your failures are not worthy of undue concern and worry since they are as natural as life itself. If you haven't failed, you haven't started.

Step Four. Develop a healthy love—of yourself! Have you discovered that it's okay to love yourself? In his book *The Art of Loving*, Erich Fromm states, "If an individual is able to love productively, he loves himself too; if he can love *only* others, he cannot love at all."[2]

When the Lord was asked, "What is the greatest commandment?" he said, "You are to love your neighbor, as you love yourself." He didn't say love your neighbor *instead* of yourself, but *as* yourself.

Self-love is not an exercise in ego-building. It is the realization that what you are is of great value and that you need care and nurture. People are capable of loving others in direct proportion to their ability to love themselves. This, of course, means a positive and healthy personal respect—not a narcissistic, egocentric, selfish love.

Step Five. Find someone who needs your help. Observers of human behavior have learned that people with low self-esteem are almost always self-centered and preoccupied with their own thoughts and actions. Instead of asking, "What can I do for you?" they ask, "What do you think of me?" They constantly look outside of themselves for a source of validation.

Today, find someone who needs your help and offer whatever talents you have. The satisfaction that results will be an important building block to a transformed self-esteem.

Step Six. Deliberately change your behavior. A great leap forward in self-perception can result from a planned action. For example, the decision to begin a daily ten-minute program of physical exercise soon produces renewed energy that affects your productivity. A weight-loss plan can give the same self-confidence.

One man decided that he was going to spend an entire day thinking tall and standing tall. Someone told him to simply "reach up with the top of your head." When he began to demonstrate an erect posture, he instantly perceived himself as a more confident and commanding person.

Step Seven. Choose a creative challenge. Building self-confidence has a direct effect on your self-esteem. You can do this by taking on a creative challenge.

Any driving instructor can tell you stories of people in their sixties and seventies who learned to drive for the first time. Passing the test was more than a personal achievement; it boosted their self-worth.

What happens to individuals can also happen to nations. History proves that immediately following a military victory, an enormous sense of pride sweeps the entire country. The effects are felt at every level of society.

Step Eight. Get comfortable with compliments. Have you learned the importance of accepting praise? Many people seem incapable of simply saying "Thank you" when they are praised for a job well done. Instead, they explain how it could have been done better or they minimize their own effort. Only you can grant yourself the permission to accept acclaim.

It's equally vital to become comfortable with criticism. Why is it that we can receive ninety-nine compliments, but one suggestion for improvement erases them all? And why do we assume that the person making the criticism is out to destroy us? In most cases, the comment we find offensive is nothing more than a genuine expression of friendship designed to help us improve.

Remember, the words others say about us are not personal until we *choose* to make them personal.

Step Nine. Revalue your worth. A piece of paper coming out of the presses of the US Treasury can be worth either $1 or $1,000. It depends on the message that is printed on it.

The prodigal son would learn an important lesson when he returned to his father. He spoke the self-defeating words, "I am . . . no longer worthy to be called your son" (Luke 15:21).

What was the father's response? "Bring the best robe and put it on him." It drastically transformed the son's perception of his place in the family. The father saw the son as unproductive, but worthy. It is self-worth that makes a profitable and productive life possible.

Avoid saying or even thinking, "I'm not worthy." You probably have much more to celebrate than to condemn. When you hum a tune, you're not merely singing—*you are the song.*

Step Ten. See a brand-new picture. Dr. Maxwell Maltz, in his book *Psycho-Cybernetics*, tells how some people who underwent plastic surgery suddenly developed a new and inspiring self-image. It wasn't so much that they were changed, but that they *believed* in their new attractiveness, and their belief affected their behavior.[3]

Your self-image doesn't happen by accident. The very word *image* implies that it is something you form or deform *yourself*. See yourself the way you *want* to be, not the way you don't want to be.

If you close your eyes and think, "I refuse to see a six-foot rab-bit," what do you see? If you constantly say to yourself, "I refuse to think about my failures," that is automatically what you will focus on. Whatever dominates your cognitive processes will dominate your life, whether it is positive or negative.

As Johann von Goethe said long ago, "Treat people as if they were what they ought to be, and you help them to become what they are capable of being." If it can happen in the way we treat oth-ers, it can happen in the way we treat ourselves.

Serita and Johnny

Our self-worth is often based on what others think of us and how they have treated us in the past. What takes place when our "value" has suddenly been changed? Here's what happened long ago on an island in the Pacific.

A young lady named Serita lived on the island of Kittywattie where the custom was that when a young man was ready to take a wife, he bartered with the father as to how many cows should be exchanged for her. A beautiful wife cost between four to six cows. An average wife was worth three.

Serita was not strikingly beautiful. She had stooped shoulders, her hair was always uncombed, and her clothes were ragged. Sam-uel, the girl's father, had already made up his mind. He thought, "I'm going to ask two cows for Serita, but I'd be willing to settle for one."

On a nearby island lived Johnny Lingo, the richest man in his community. He gained his wealth by being a shrewd trader. After many visits to Kittywattie, he announced that he was in love with Serita. No one could believe it.

Johnny came to her father and what he said was shocking. "Sir, I would like Serita to be my wife, and I am offering eight cows."

The word spread through the island with lightning speed. "Eight cows?" one villager exclaimed. "Johnny's either crazy or blind!"

Another remarked, "Why would a smart trader offer eight cows for a woman he could have for one?"

Johnny knew a great secret. And it was not long until his bride knew it, too. Until that moment, Kittywattie had treated Serita as a "one-cow woman," and it shaped her personality.

But to Johnny Lingo, she was an "eight-cow woman," and that is exactly what she became. The moment Serita realized her newfound worth, she instantly blossomed into the most beautiful woman in all the islands.

What Is Your Value?

What would an appraiser estimate as your worth? If you were a wristwatch, your value would depend on whether the words on the face read "Timex" or "Rolex." If you were a painting, it would depend on whether you were offered at a London flea market or a Paris art gallery. The value is not in the metal parts of the watch or the paint on the canvas. It is the perceived value that makes the difference.

Just as a store clerk places a new price tag on merchandise, you can examine and attach value to yourself. In doing so, however, don't think about your physical attributes. Think about who created you and the quality of his workmanship. Then you will have an idea of your value, and you "treat right" that which you value. By immediately acting upon the "Ten Steps to a Transformed Self-Esteem," you can face the world—and yourself—with a bold new confidence about your future.

a transformed thought-life

Recently, a man at a baseball game was rushed to the hospital after claiming he had been poisoned by a soft drink purchased at the stadium.

Unfortunately, the stadium announcer told the crowd, "Ladies and gentlemen, we regret to inform you that our concession stand is now closed. A gentleman is being taken to the hospital by ambulance and is being treated for suspected poisoning from soda from the soft drink dispenser."

Almost as quickly as those words had been spoken, people began to complain of symptoms that might be caused by poisoning, and shuttles began making trips to the local hospital. It turned out that the first man did not have any trace of poison. The power of thought produced the pain.

Dr. Albert Cliffe, a well-known chemist, wrote in his book, *Lessons in Successful Living,* "If you are afraid of a draft, then you will get the cold you were afraid of. The draft never gave you a cold, but your belief in it will certainly demonstrate the cold in your system."[1]

The power of your mind is awesome. Medical science has discovered that the brain produces a chemical that can actually stop your heart, lungs, and the mental processes all at the same time. And it is controlled by your thoughts. Repeatedly, we hear the stories of elderly people dying, only to learn that their lifelong partner passed away within days, even hours, of their death. The power of a "death wish" is beyond our comprehension.

The annals of medical research leave no doubt that mental health and physical well-being are directly linked. Our reactions to other people play a vital role, too.

In Dr. S. I. McMillen's book, *None of These Diseases*, in a chapter titled "The High Cost of Getting Even," he illustrates how physical maladies including ulcers, high blood pressure, and strokes are connected to harboring resentment and hatred toward others. He says, "It might be written on many thousands of death certificates that the victim died of 'grudgitis.'" Dr. McMillen describes how hating a person enslaves the one who hates.

> The moment I start hating a man I become his slave. I cannot enjoy my work anymore because he even controls my thoughts. My resentments produce too many stress hormones in my body; I become fatigued after only a few hours of work. . . . The man I hate may be miles from my bedroom, but more cruel than any slave driver he whips my thoughts into such a frenzy that my innerspring mattress becomes a rack of torture. I really must acknowledge that I am a slave to every man on whom I pour out my wrath.[2]

Is it any wonder that hospitals are filled to capacity and that many physicians are too busy to accept new patients?

Your body gives you expression in the physical world, but is influenced by the content of your mind. That being the case, in order to live in good health, you must think good thoughts.

Examine Your "Self-Talk"

People's behavior, almost without exception, is determined by perception. What do they think about? What do they talk about? Research indicates that most of the average person's talk about self is negative. And since everything produces after its kind, you don't have to be a prophet to predict the future for these people.

For many, constant self-doubt results in a state of depression. It is a mental condition brought on by what you think about *you*, not what you think about other people or events. The never-ending diet of negative thoughts creates a powerful illusion of truth that becomes all-consuming.

What's important to know, however, is that feelings are not facts. Instead, they are simply a mirror of the way we are thinking. But here is the problem: Our unrealistic emotions feel just as valid and realistic as genuine feelings, so we automatically attribute truth to them. It is only when we deliberately step back a few paces from our problems that we begin to have a clear view of the forces at work.

Can we truly gain control over our thought-life? Is our mind something to be managed? Or is it off limits? So often we tend to shun anything connected to the mind, because of the connection with the occult, eastern religions, or metaphysics. But we'll never experience the turn-around we seek without a conscious decision to take charge of our thoughts.

The "strongholds" that work against us do not come in the form of a job, the economy, or a critic. No! They are in the mind, thoughts, and imagination. The apostle Paul wrote to the church at Rome,

"For to be carnally minded is death; but to be spiritually minded is life and peace" (Rom. 8:6).

What should be the focus of our thoughts?

> Whatever things are true, whatever things are noble, whatever things are just, whatever things are pure, whatever things are lovely, whatever things are of good report, if there is any virtue and if there is anything praiseworthy, meditate on these things. (Phil. 4:8)

The Law of Mental Action

The law of thermodynamics says that for every action there is an equal and opposite reaction. There is also a law of mental action, stated most aptly in the Bible, "For as he thinks in his heart, so is he" (Prov. 23:7). In other words, our thought process is not only centered in the conscious mind but goes much deeper. It comes from the heart—from our inner self.

The four steps of transforming thoughts into positive action are these: knowing, thinking, saying, and doing. In this chapter, we're dealing with the first two.

The old adage, "You are what you eat," also applies to your mind, "You are what you think!" And what you are starts with what you know. Wrong information produces wrong thinking, which produces wrong words or actions.

How long has it been since you reacted to a problem by saying, "I'm going to totally concentrate on this one issue"? This is how creative ideas develop, and with practice, they will begin to flow quickly. H. L. Mencken wrote, "My guess is that well over 80 percent of the human race goes through life without having a single original thought." Or, as Thomas Edison said, "There is no expedient to which a man will not go to avoid the real labor of thinking."

Many people's thought processes are shallow and lead to faulty conclusions. For example, people believe that because something happened once, it will occur again and again. After washing their car, it rains. What is their response? "It happens every time!" Or, someone treats them badly and they say, "Nobody likes me!" Beware of the tendency to overgeneralize or use faulty logic.

It's time to consider treating your mind as the treasure it really is. Your thoughts contain life's most valued possessions—health, abundance, compassion, and love.

Start to creatively "activate" your mind to solve the problems you face. Begin by getting yourself out of a mental rut.

A New Perspective

Einstein did no experiments and gathered no new information before he created the theory of relativity. He simply found a new way of looking at information that had been available to everyone else. It was only *after* he discovered his famous theory that experiments confirming it were done.

One of history's most important medical discoveries happened when Edward Jenner stopped trying to find out why people got smallpox. Instead, he began to investigate why women who milked cows apparently did not. From his discovery, that harmless cowpox gave protection against the dreaded smallpox, came the vaccination that ended the world's smallpox plague. It has been said that there are no incurable diseases, only incurable people.

In his fascinating book, *New Think*, Edward De Bono promotes the idea of expanding our creativity by lateral thinking. He says, "You cannot dig a hole in a different place by digging the same hole deeper." Vertical thinking simply keeps digging in the same location. "Lateral thinking," says De Bono, "is concerned with digging a hole in another place."[3]

The genius inside can be awakened by consciously breaking the habit of knee-jerk reactions to what comes your way. The rewards of creativity aren't the exclusive rights of artists or inventors. You have the power of uninhibited thought that can give your life a totally new dimension.

Starting now, make a commitment that you will spend some time every day exercising, expanding, and applying the potential of your mind.

a new look at your goals

It's a well-known fact that if you don't know where you're headed, you'll never recognize your destination when you arrive. For the vast majority of people, a goal is nebulous and fuzzy, more like a dense fog than a concrete and succinctly stated objective. It would be great to think that we all have the necessary training to design master plans for our lives, but that isn't the case. The tragedy of our educational system is that we can attend school for eighteen years and never have one hour of instruction in goal setting.

Bryan Tracy, author of *The Psychology of Achievement*, says, "According to the best research, less than 3 percent of Americans have written goals, and less than 1 percent review and rewrite their goals on a daily basis."[1]

What about you? How would you respond to the question, "What do you plan to be doing ten years from today?"

Charles F. Kettering, the inventor of the automobile self-starter and many industrial devices, knew the importance of looking ahead. He said, "My interest is in the future because I am going to spend the rest of my life there."[2]

Goal setting is not the exclusive domain of the entrepreneur or the high achiever. It's not a God-given talent but a learned skill that anyone can master. Most people, however, only scratch the surface of their potential because they avoid visualizing their future.

In this hour, you are being asked to focus on your ambitions and aspirations. Here are seven specific targets.

Target One: My Goal Is Specific

At the age of fifteen, John Goddard set down 127 goals for his life. By age forty-seven, he had achieved 103 of them. As a result of clear objectives, Goddard explored the Nile, climbed Mount Kilimanjaro, learned to fly an airplane, and photographed Africa's Victoria Falls.

What was his secret? Each of Goddard's goals was both action-oriented and specific. For example, the list included: "to *become* an Eagle Scout, to *type fifty* words *a minute,* to *dive* to *forty feet* holding my breath for *two- and one-half minutes* underwater, to *play* the flute and violin, to *learn* jujitsu, to *high-jump five feet,* to *build* my own telescope, to *watch* a fire-walking ceremony in Bali."[3]

Goddard, who became a celebrated adventurer and lecturer, lived a life that others only dream about. It happened because his goals were precise.

You don't need to begin with 127 targets—just a few clear objectives will do. What *is* important is that the targets at which you are aiming are specific.

Target Two: My Goal Is Measurable

Many people confuse a goal with a purpose. If you say, "I want to be happy," or, "I want to have lots of money," it's rather difficult to determine the moment of victory.

The clearest goals are measured by quantity, not quality. It is important to aim for things that have a high purpose, but being able to mark your progress in relation to the purpose is almost impossible.

Some people make a New Year's resolution that says, "I'm going to spend more time reading this year." A more measurable goal would be, "This year, I'm going to read two chapters of a book every day." Only then can their achievement be quantified and measured.

As you begin to formulate your objectives, ask yourself, "Is this goal measurable?"

Target Three: My Goal Is Challenging, Yet Achievable

The goals you set are to be demanding, yet doable. You may not be able to achieve your goal in one hour or one day. In fact, if you can, it's not much of a goal. You may also fail at achieving your goal for a while before you succeed. But remember, your failures can be your best teachers.

To the achieving person, failure is viewed as a vital element in ultimate success. When you fall down as a little child, it doesn't keep you from learning to walk. When you bite your tongue, it doesn't stop you from eating. Achievement takes a willingness to put your face to the wind and move forward. You don't make great strides by following the path of least resistance.

A football player who received the coveted Heisman Trophy said, "I've waited many years for this day." But that was a modest understatement. Actually, he had *worked* many years for that moment.

The victory, however, is always worth it all. As quarterback Joe Namath said, "When you win, nothing hurts."

Orville and Wilbur Wright's flying machine didn't zoom off into the blue Carolina skies on the first attempt. Their little twelve-horsepower, two-wing plane was in the air only three and one-half seconds. They spent the next two days repairing the damage from the disastrous landing. Then, on December 17, 1903, they flew their wood-frame and cotton-cloth contraption for twelve seconds. Then fifteen seconds. Then fifty-nine. And the feat was etched in the annals of world history. But what good was an airplane that could rise a few feet off the ground for just one minute? Kitty Hawk was only the start. It took years to perfect an aircraft that would fly high enough and long enough to be practical. The saga was one of trial and error, with many more failures than triumphs.

Be sure that your goal is not to repeat something you have already achieved, but to reach for a new challenge.

Target Four: It Is My Goal, Not Someone Else's

In setting the agenda for your future, make certain that your objectives are self-produced. Just because your father or your boss wants something, or because you are good at it, does not mean it should become your goal.

Every day the news is filled with stories of young people who fall victim to drugs, alcohol, and moral failure because they allow peer pressure to replace self-determination. They know the difference between right and wrong, but they follow the advice of others instead of their own hearts. When you feel it on the inside, your chances of success are improved enormously.

It is also dangerous to allow goals to be prescribed by circumstances. The environment of your youth or the current status of your checking account should not be allowed to limit your aspirations.

When setting goals, do some creative thinking to expand the boundary line of your possibilities. The moment you visualize yourself in a new situation, a profound transformation takes place in your actions. The link between expectations and personal achievement cannot be denied.

When people measure progress, however, it is important to ask the right questions. Instead of, "How am I doing against the competition?" try asking, "How far have I come since the last time I tried?"

It's *your* advancement that is the gauge of your success.

Target Five: All of My Goals Reinforce Each Other

It's a rare and dangerous thing to have only one goal. A balanced life should include a blueprint for achievement in your entire arena of experience—personal, family, financial, academic, physical, and spiritual.

Many people have objectives that are incompatible. For example, they are ruled by a ruthless business philosophy that says, "I'll become the president of my company, and no one's going to stand in my way." Then, at church, they profess to believe, "Do unto others as you would have them do unto you."

If you want to assure ongoing and rapid progress toward any *single* objective, make certain that *all* of your stated goals are headed in the same direction.

Target Six: My Goal Includes a Plan to Achieve It

A stated destination is meaningless without a road map that shows you the best route. Once you are on the way, anything can happen. Suddenly a detour sign may appear, but it doesn't stop you if you know where you're headed.

After you have determined your goal, devise a specific plan to see it come to pass. The "A, B, C" or "1, 2, 3" lists may seem time-consuming, but they are the guide to your future.

Here's the important point: *Your goal may seldom change, but your plan should always be flexible.* If plan one doesn't work, don't panic. You have discovered vital information. Now it's time to try plan two. As Peter Drucker says, "Long-range planning does not deal with future decisions, but with the future of present decisions."

Make sure your strategy includes a timetable for action. Without it, you'll never begin. Some people say they'll reach their goal when they get the kids through college or when the mortgage is paid off on their house.

The great satisfaction is not in reaching your final goal, but in the joy of the journey. Don't worry if your target seems to keep moving like a mirage in the desert. Enjoy the achievement of every small mile marker on the scenic road you travel. Begin each day with the challenge, "This is the day which the LORD hath made; we will rejoice and be glad in it" (Ps. 118:24).

Target Seven: I Will Write Down My Goal

The quickest way to see your dreams and desires become tangible is to find pen and paper and begin to write. The moment you *see* what you are seeking—even on that small piece of paper—it takes on a physical appearance.

In his book, *The Self-Talk Solution*, behavioral researcher Shad Helmstetter gives specific words we need to say regarding goal setting. They include, "Anytime I want to make a change or achieve anything in my life, I write it down, along with my plan to accomplish the goal and when I will achieve it. In this way I turn each of my goals into action."

He also asks that we say, "By writing out my goals, I am actually writing my own script for the story of my future. By following my specific action plan, I turn my dreams into reality."[4]

Start writing!

The seven targets for goal setting are meaningless unless you put them into action. For each one, try reading the objective aloud and see how it applies to your written goal. Most important, do something specific every day that brings you closer to your objective. By looking at the "bull's-eye," rather than the distractions, you're halfway home. A winner is not problem-oriented, but solution-oriented.

In the twenty-four hours called today, you have 86,400 seconds at your disposal. How will you use them? Will the ticks of the clock be squandered by daydreaming, idleness, and indecision? Or will they be filled with the excitement of reaching your goal? A sign hanging over the counter of a gun shop said, "Having a great aim in life is important. So is knowing when to pull the trigger."

Ready. Aim. Fire!

great expectations

Do you believe that tomorrow is going to be better than today? Your response reveals much more than a simple one-word answer. If you harbor a basic fear about the future, it will soon permeate every aspect of your behavior and personality.

What happens when the weather forecaster on the Friday night news predicts storm and rain? Thousands of people change their plans for the weekend. Some people change more than their plans. Although at the moment the skies may be clear, these people suddenly become sullen, moody, and depressed at the prospect of what may be coming.

Stockbrokers know that the investor who is worried about tomorrow goes broke playing the market. They have seen plenty of people take huge losses on stocks because they had no faith that the price would ever bounce back. They know that the person who has constant faith in the future will wind up rich because he or she is consistent. They buy when it's high and buy when it's low. Over the long haul the person accumulates large quantities of stock and the value is enormous. It is a well-known fact that it takes a certain type to make it in the market. You've got to believe in the future.

Expectation triggers both conscious and unconscious behaviors that produce anticipated results. Psychologists see people every day who are actually expecting the worst to happen. In many cases, it is their expectation that is the real problem. Here are some of the things patients say:

"I don't know what it is, but I know I've got a serious health condition."

"Financially, we're just not going to make it."

"I just don't know how this marriage is going to last."

Dominantly negative expectations can sabotage your health, wealth, and happiness.

Seeing and Hoping

Some people create a facade of confidence that is purely cosmetic. When you begin to think about the future, the real you—*the person inside*—starts to show. As you will discover, expectancy is a dynamic force that plays a great role in life.

Remember that there is no such thing as a hopeless situation—only hopeless people. Before you can *realize* a positive outcome, you must learn to *visualize* it—to the degree that it becomes consciously pronounced in your thought processes.

An outstanding swimmer attempted to cross the choppy waters of the English Channel. Mile after mile she swam the cold, rough, forbidding waters. Toward the end of her exhausting swim, she encountered a dense fog that drastically limited her visibility. She was only a half mile from her goal, but she called for the lifeboat and abandoned her attempt. Reflecting on the experience she said, "If

I could just have seen the land, I wouldn't have given up." Limited visibility caused her to fail by only a small margin. While we cannot always physically see our goal, we must develop the ability to visualize it by faith.

In a study conducted by Dr. Hazel Markus of the University of Michigan, psychologists determined that self-improvement can be enhanced by developing the ability to "elaborate the self you want to become, to make it as vivid and specific as you possibly can in imagining how you will look and feel."

For example, before playing in a softball game, spend some time alone "seeing yourself" standing at the plate, swinging the bat, and striking the ball. Or, as a fielder, see yourself catching the ball as it comes toward you.

Like so many techniques that can transform our lives, visualization is a learned skill. It is something we can experience by doing it once—then again and again until it becomes a positive routine that is deeply seated in our outlook, attitude, and conduct.

When we mentally "see" the future, it has a powerful effect on our lives. As O. S. Marden wrote, "There is no medicine like hope, no incentive so great, and no tonic so powerful as expectation of something tomorrow."

When people form a visual image of their desired behavior, an improvement in actual performance usually follows. A study by Deborah Feltzer and C. A. Riessinger reported in the *Journal of Sport and Exercise Psychology* reveals that individuals participating in sports who use visualization have significantly higher scores than those using only feedback after each performance.[1]

Once you see that your perceptions determine your behavior, you can begin immediately to shift your focus from your actions to your attitudes. When you change in your *mind's* eye, you see things differently with your *physical* eye. Soon the view from inside becomes manifest in the way you walk, the words you speak, and the manner in which people respond to you.

A Sense of Wonder

If we could magically return to the age of two, we would be amazed at our view of the world. That's when we were doing original research into the nature of the universe. We saw our surroundings in such an unusual way that it was beyond description. Great poets maintain a sense of wonder and are able to communicate it. The people we call geniuses somehow have avoided putting the creative, wondering child within them to sleep.

There are two types of people in the world—magnetized and demagnetized, although we probably all start our life magnetized. People magnetized with the power of positive expectation actually attract success, happiness, and the achievement of their goals with their faith and confidence. But if they don't use the magnetism, they lose it.

Demagnetized people don't attract any such things. Opportunities come to them, but they sit there like a heavy piece of demagnetized metal. They say, "I might fail. I might lose money. People will laugh at me."

You know that you cannot move forward by looking in a rearview mirror. One of the great lessons from ancient Israel is to "remember Lot's wife." She looked back and turned into a pillar of salt. The moment you allow past experiences to dominate either your present or your future, you are headed for major problems. Many people have been carrying the same old baggage for ten or twenty years. Finally, the weight of it zaps their energy and they permanently collapse under the load.

Some people go through their entire lives with the mistaken notion that what they are doing is all they are capable of doing. To them, existence is based totally on experience and circumstance. They don't even know their awareness is limited. As a result, they cannot see beyond their problems. Unless they change their mental conditioning, they will live out their lives with the potential for greatness still locked up inside of them.

What you believed yesterday is so powerful that it made you the person you are today. By the same token, if you dwell on what you are now, you will not move beyond your present self. It is only by focusing on your future self—by seeing *beyond* what you are—that you can realize your great potential. The apostle Paul told the people at Corinth, "Old things have passed away; behold, all things have become new" (2 Cor. 5:17).

Believe You Can

It's time to challenge yourself to grow by increasing the level of your belief. Take a pen and paper and write at least ten statements starting with the words, "I believe I can . . ." For example, you may write, "I believe I can write a poem worthy of publication." Then take the next step. Actually *attempt* to do what you believe is possible. Belief is the fuel that allows you to fly. Go ahead, venture to do something greater and higher than you've ever done before.

These words of Robert Schuller are worth heeding, "I would rather attempt to do something great and fail, than attempt to do nothing and succeed."

We live in what human resources consultant Les Brown calls the era of the "Three C's": accelerated *change*, overwhelming *complexity*, and tremendous *competition*. Most of us, most of the time, seem overwhelmed by what is happening around us. We feel as if we are in the eye of a hurricane, and we're afraid to move because we may be flattened by the forces whirling all around us. In such a situation, however, there is only one hope. We can't look to the right, to the left, or even below us. Our only clear hope is to remember what God has already done in our lives and to focus on the potential he has given us.

"Keep looking ahead" should become a personal philosophy that defines our approach to every encounter. If there is one strategy that spells success, it is the ability to consistently develop scenarios with positive outcomes. Someone once said, "It is perhaps insane to live with a dream, but it is madness to live without one."

Centuries ago people believed the earth was flat. Their belief restricted their spirit of adventure. Imagine mothers in those days telling their children, "Don't move too far from the shoreline or you'll fall off the earth." Unfortunately, many parents send similar messages to their children today—words that instill apprehension and anxiety about the future. So often, dreams of discovery are dashed before they have a chance to develop. But those who feel free to choose can reestablish their lost confidence. They cannot only wade out into the water, but they can launch a ship that will lead to a wondrous new world.

As children, our identity and self-image were formed by the definition of the significant others in our lives, usually our mothers and fathers. That definition deeply affects everything we believe about ourselves and our ability to relate to our surroundings. There must come a time, however, when we realize that we can no longer live by someone else's definition. Ultimately, we must each take the necessary steps to reshape our lives. We can choose what we discard and what we keep, what we bury and what we believe.

It is not the experiences of your life that determine your outcome. *It is the meaning you attach to each experience.* This is why we must constantly challenge the validity of our perceptions or "belief systems." For example, studies of battered women show that they are often more unhappy when not being harmed. Why? They perceive being battered as "getting attention." Again and again they demonstrate that "being noticed" is preferable to not being hit. Behavior does not change until our belief system is challenged and changed.

What Do You See?

Have you heard the phrase, "What you see is who you'll be"? It's true. People who don't like who they are begin to change the moment they start to see themselves differently. It is time to take an honest look at the "expectation factor" that so powerfully steers the course of your life. You can either continue to react to doubt and fear in a knee-jerk, automatic manner that leaves you lifeless and dejected, or you can deliberately alter your behavior. You may say, "I can't help how I feel about the future. It's just the way I am!"

Fortunately, you are not held totally captive by negative circumstances, poor environment, or even the fatalistic beliefs of others. Just as God has granted you the power to live, he has given you the power to *change*.

Today, choose just *one* specific area of your life that is causing you worry or fear. It may be anything from an upcoming visit to the dentist to an employment performance review. By making a deliberate choice to focus on a positive outcome, you can change your entire outlook concerning that upcoming event. Suddenly you are relaxed, even smiling, about something that could have caused you great anxiety and sleepless nights.

If your outlook can be transformed in just one aspect of life, the potential exists for change in *all* areas of life.

Why leave your future in the hands of fate? Expectation can make it great!

a major attitude adjustment

When you drive to the service department of your automobile dealership, the manager wants to know, "Do you need a major overhaul or just some minor adjustments?"

You can ask yourself the same question about the way you view life. What needs changing? It doesn't usually take an observation from a professional to determine your general attitude toward life. You already know whether you're an optimist or a pessimist, an introvert or an extrovert, good-humored or serious. You may not be on the extreme end of any scale, but you know your general tendencies.

For some people, forecasting negative scenarios becomes a normal way of life, a major part of their outlook and personality. It could be said that optimists and pessimists both expect their dreams to come true. But pessimists' dreams are nightmares.

What is your basic response to the events that surround you? And what will it take to see that response change? A newspaper editor in Idaho told his housekeeper one morning, "I think we're going to have a great crop of potatoes this year."

"No way," said the housekeeper. "I think it's going to be terrible."

The editor was thinking about her remark when he wrote an unsigned editorial predicting an excellent outlook for the potato crop. That night when he got home, the housekeeper was waiting for him at the door with the paper in her hand. "I was wrong," she said. "It says right here in the paper that the crop will be excellent this year."

This housekeeper believed anything she saw in print. She didn't trust her own perceptions that the potato crop was going to be bad, but went with the "outside" evidence. She did adjust her *opinion*, but that's not the same as adjusting her *attitude*.

The Source of Our Attitudes

In this hour you are being asked to take an inventory of your attitude, the way you respond to people, objects, institutions, events, or issues. If you detect an enduring predisposition to behave or react in a negative manner, you've suddenly found an area of your life worth changing. Fortunately, your attitudes are not permanently fixed like the pigment of your skin or the color of your eyes. You can drastically change your response to life by making a conscious choice to do so.

Psychologist Peter Ashworth, writing in the *Journal of Phenomenological Psychology*, says that attitude is "an intentional phenomenon" that is a part of our "consciousness" and "awareness." Therefore, it is something we have control over and can change.[1]

Let's begin by examining the *source* of our attitudes. There are three major origins: culture, family, and personal experience. More often than not, we tend to reflect the prevailing perspective of the culture in which we grow up. Also, many attitudes are passed on from generation to generation within the family structure. But we are not totally the products of our childhoods. Research shows that many of our attitudes are developed as adults on the basis of personal experience. We are continually bombarded with propaganda, suggestions from government, business, and educational institutions that influence our outlook and behavior.

It should come as no surprise that most people see the dark side of daily life. We're conditioned to it. The nightly news begins with "Good evening," and that's usually the last good thing we will hear.

The problem is that when we develop a prevailing attitude, it colors everything we see. We automatically and instantly categorize and classify things. For example, someone with a favorable opinion toward the Right to Life movement is more likely to respond favorably to others who hold the same view and to disregard negative characteristics of people associated with the cause.

Or, a person who believes all New Yorkers are obnoxious and aggressive will have the same negative response to people from the Big Apple, regardless of their behavior.

How we experience the *outer* world is determined by our *inner* world. We do not see the world as it actually is, but the way we perceive it to be. Depression, for example, is not something that happens to us but is our response to what we perceive. The noted reality therapist William Glasser says people are "depressing" or "angrying" themselves as opposed to being angry or being depressed.

Your Basic Disposition

The noted Swiss psychoanalyst and founder of analytical psychology, Carl Jung, classified people according to their dispositions. The basic types are the *introvert*, who is inwardly oriented, and the *extrovert*, who is outwardly oriented. According to Jung, the introvert withdraws into himself—particularly in times of stress. The introvert tends to be self-sufficient and task-oriented, while the extrovert needs interaction with people.

No matter what your basic disposition, you have the ability to change your attitudes. Perhaps you have said, "I wish that I could be more outgoing," or "I wish that I could see the bright side of things." For many, the desire is frustrated by a lack of confidence. Here are some obvious signs of it:

You haven't done anything new lately.

You look for excuses to avoid a challenge.

You fail to accept responsibility.

Your "nerves" are showing.

If your boss calls, you think, "What did I do wrong?" instead of, "Thank God my raise is coming through."

The process of change begins when you choose to be confident about the future. *Con* means "*with*," and *fidel* means "*faith*." Confidence, then, simply means "*living with faith*."

Noah built the ark without a Black & Decker power saw and without a building permit from the local government. But that's not all. Noah packed it with eagles and elephants, squirrels and scorpions, and took a forty-day vacation in a rainstorm. That's optimism!

Your commitment to confidence, hope, and positive outcomes provides a strong basis for action.

There's an old story about two Texans who were bragging about who was the best bear hunter. One said, "I can hunt a bear with just my knife." The other said, "I don't even need that. I just use my hands." To determine who was the bravest hunter, they took a trip to Alaska and found a remote cabin. The second man who bragged he didn't need anything walked about two hundred yards from the cabin and suddenly faced a humongous bear standing on his hind feet. The man turned and ran, with the bear snapping at his posterior with every step. When he reached the cabin, he threw open the door and sailed against the wall. The bear was right behind him.

The man said to his friend with the knife, "You skin this one; I'm going out for another."

The hunter who bragged about using only his hands was optimistic, but not realistic. It was the man with the knife who lived to tell the tale.

As former British Prime Minister Harold Wilson once said, "I'm an optimist, but I'm an optimist who carries a raincoat."

The decision to deliberately choose hope instead of fear may at first seem "out of character," but it is worth the effort. That decision begins with an awareness that you have a choice. If you are not aware of what is happening, you can fall so deeply into the trap of negative thinking that your entire life is affected. The French writer Robert Mallet said, "Many pessimists end up by desiring the things they fear, in order to prove that they are right."

A lady said, "I have to look up to see bottom." Then she realized, "That's okay. I have to look up to see the top too." Remember, there was only one window in Noah's ark—it was up at the top. It's perfectly normal to look at the problem, but we must also be ready to view the solution.

There is a wonderful story of Jesus in the midst of the multitude, looking up into a tree to see a man by the name of Zacchaeus. The Lord singled him out and declared that he would go to his home. It was not because of his altitude but because of his attitude.

Attitude of Gratitude

In our process of personal change and transformation, there is one area in which we can see consistent results. It is the way in which we show appreciation to others for their kindness. It's called an attitude of gratitude.

Americans have been celebrating Thanksgiving Day ever since December 13, 1621, when Governor William Bradford decreed a three-day feast to give thanks for a good harvest and new hope. Even with the problems that surround us, there is still plenty for which to be thankful.

Barnett Gibson, in his book *Happiness Day and Night*, says, "It doesn't matter how full life may have filled your fortunate hands; if you have no gratitude, you reside on spiritual 'skid row.'"

One thing is certain—you can't harbor heartfelt gratitude and depression at the same time. Ingratitude produces emotional paralysis, while a grateful heart releases a continual abundance of positive results.

The apostle Paul said, "In everything give thanks; for this is the will of God in Christ Jesus for you" (1 Thess. 5:18).

The Key to Change

Whether it is in the area of being thankful, optimistic, enthusiastic, or outgoing, the key to change is to realize that an existing attitude is not something you are "stuck" with. Millions of negative people have reversed their "polarity." They have substituted yes for no, and hope for nope!

Viktor Frankl, in his compelling book *Man's Search for Meaning*, said, "Everything can be taken from a person but one thing: the last of human freedoms—to choose one's attitude in any given set of circumstances and to choose one's own way."[2] Frankl survived the German prison camps by clinging to a personal belief that love is the ultimate and highest goal to which humans can aspire.

Any experienced counselor will tell you that the attitude of the therapist is often more important than technique, knowledge, or theory. Whether your objective is to help others or to help yourself, the decision to elevate your attitude is vital. You can begin now by consciously verbalizing and demonstrating a positive outlook. Being an optimist does not mean that you deny the problem. It means that you accept the obstacle as a challenge in preparation for a positive outcome.

You may ask, "Where am I to begin?" Start today by complimenting those around you. Go ahead and say something encouraging to the server at a restaurant, to the postal clerk, to one of your fellow employees.

When someone asks, "What do you think will happen?" take a split second to evaluate your response, and then phrase your answer in the positive. When you decide that optimism is going to become your new lifestyle, prepare yourself for a harvest of happiness.

choose your new team

One of the most spectacular mountain ascents on record was the assault on Mt. Everest by Sir Edmund Hillary and his native guide, Tenzing Norgay. While they were descending from that forbidding peak, Hillary suddenly lost his footing. Tenzing Norgay instantly dug his axe into the ice, held the rope tight, and kept both of them from falling. When they were interviewed by newsmen, Tenzing Norgay refused to take special credit for saving Hillary's life. He said it was just a normal, routine part of his job. Then he added, "Mountain climbers *always* help each other."

Every day we face our own Mt. Everest as part of our great expedition of life. The progress we make can be greatly advanced by those we select to join us on the journey.

In this hour you are being asked to carefully examine your team, the people you turn to for help in this great adventure.

How are they influencing your progress? Are they encouraging you to make great strides forward? Or are they constantly pulling you down?

Many people find they are surrounded by entrapments instead of relationships. It's sad but true that a great many human ties are based on possessiveness, guilt, dominion, and control.

Psychiatrist Fritz Perls in his book, *In and Out of the Garbage Pail*, speaks of two types of people: "T" types (Toxic), and "N" types (Nurturing). This distinction is important to remember when you are choosing your friends. Toxic people will drain your energy and leave you fatigued, whereas the nurturing type will encourage your growth with support and confidence.[1]

Your Basic Team

Ask yourself this question, "Who are the five most powerful people in my life?" Then, as you reflect on each person, make a realistic assessment of his or her contribution to your well-being. If four out of five on your list are positive, upbeat, encouraging people, you may consider yourself extremely fortunate. If the opposite is true, you're in a crisis situation that needs immediate action.

Any good automobile mechanic will tell you that your engine will be at peak performance when every spark plug, every piston, and every valve is in perfect working condition. Just one defective part can cause havoc. The same is true about the people you run with.

You may ask, "What should I do about someone who is constantly telling me why I will fail or is criticizing every decision I make?" Perhaps that person is someone you are very close to, a family member or a lifelong friend. It is important to use diplomacy and tact in dealing with toxic people.

You should not make a rash decision to suddenly disassociate yourself from people you realize are stumbling blocks to your future. Don't wait for everybody to agree with you. If they say they do, you can be sure they probably don't mean it. It is much better to become totally aware of their actions and respond accordingly. See people for what they truly are and learn to appreciate both their strengths and weaknesses. Accept their positive actions and then objectively, constructively, observe their attempts to create barriers and detours.

Here's an example. When five people tell you something can't be done, say to yourself, "I must be on the right track." Oh, they may be angry that you didn't heed their advice, but when you win, they'll say, "I knew all the time you were going to make it!"

If these five people comprise the majority of your circle of friends, you need to add one or two new people to your team. Perhaps you already know who they are—people who have a cheerful, optimistic outlook on life and who demonstrate personal growth and success. Deliberately create ways to spend as much time as possible with them.

No, you don't need to abandon your old friends. Instead, make a commitment to expand your team to include those who will help you up the mountain.

Barbra Streisand has sung it for years, "People. People who need people, are the luckiest people in the world." We need each other. Just as one part of a body needs the other parts so that it can function, so we need other people in all areas of our lives to operate at maximum capacity. We are in this life together! The key is to choose friends who will make the greatest possible contribution.

According to business consultant Jack Zufelt,

> If you want to know how to do something, talk to people who are skilled in or successful at it. If you want to go from $30,000

a year in income to $70,000, don't ask somebody who is earning only $45,000 or $50,000 to teach you. He will be able to teach you only how he got to his level.

It is not uncommon for successful entrepreneurs to pay certain employees more than they pay themselves. They know the importance of building a strong and talented team. Look closely at these words from the Bible: "He who walks with wise men will be wise, but the companion of fools will be destroyed" (Prov. 13:20).

Many people, when they are surrounded by negative forces, make the tragic mistake of becoming loners, isolating themselves from society. Instead of seeking out new centers of influence, they go into hibernation. Suddenly, their communication becomes watching endless hours of television, going to the movies, or listening to the radio. But it is all *one-way* information, which is not really communication at all.

C. S. Lewis wrote in *The Four Loves*,

> If you want to make sure of keeping your heart intact, you must give it to no one. Avoid all entanglements, lock it up safe in the coffin of selfishness. But in that coffin—safe, dark, motionless, airless—it will change. It will not be broken; it will become unbreakable and irredeemable.

The Power of Consensus

There is a much better way to live. It's surprising how much progress you can make in a short period of time by acting on a decision to tap into the power of people. How can such a change be made? It's as simple as saying, "Next week, I'm not going to eat one lunch alone. I'm going to schedule lunch every day with someone I need to know better." Pick up the phone and make those appointments.

Attempting to go it alone rarely succeeds. In the business world, results have proven again and again that the most powerful decisions that move a company forward are not those of a strong, authoritarian president. Instead they are decisions in which both the employees and management have come together to find a solution.

Warren Avis, founder of the car rental company that bears his name, demonstrated the power of a concept called "shared participation." In his book, *The Art of Sharing*, he describes how it works.

> Members of a group contribute information and suggest solutions to specific problems. These are not labeled as to their source, and solutions from persons untrained in a field are thus discussed as fully as those put forth by experts. The solution reached is a voluntary consensus of the group and most often not one of the original suggestions at all, but a new one or an amalgam that evolved out of the resulting discussions.[2]

The reason the process works is that every idea has equal weight. They are written anonymously and read out loud. There is no intimidation to accept a concept because it comes from a powerful leader. Something else also happens. When the decision is made to move forward, the chances of success are incredibly increased because the force of a group is behind it.

Do you remember the story of Captain Bligh in *Mutiny on the Bounty*? He ran his ship with an iron hand, and the fear and intimidation he exerted over his crew became intolerable.

Why did Bligh's men rebel? There were thousands of other ships at sea with similar conditions that did *not* mutiny. They rebelled because their captain did not know how to lead men. He drove them past the point of endurance. They were willing to risk death rather than continue to live under such harsh rule.

The great lessons of leadership need to be practiced on a personal level every day. The love principle works. More progress is made by a pat on the back than by a slap on the hand.

This is also true in education. Far more learning takes place through cooperation than through competition. When students are charting their own course and devising ways to make the top grade on an exam, there are only winners and losers.

On the other hand, when teams of students work together on a problem, exceptional learning can take place and everyone can win. Some contribute facts, others add logic, and still others offer creativity. Some excel in presenting the results through graphics and oral presentations. The team approach works.

Success at All Levels

Something extraordinary happens when you join forces with other people. What seems impossible for you to do alone is suddenly simple when tackled by a group pulling in the same direction. The power of encouragement is amazing. It works at all levels of life—in reaching goals, in building a business, in making friends, and in creating harmony out of chaos.

We should take seriously the words found in Scripture that tell us, "Comfort one another," "Bear one another's burdens," "Edify one another," and "Love one another." What happens when we do? "If we love one another, God abides in us, and His love has been perfected in us" (1 John 4:12).

Many years ago, John Donne wrote, "No man is an island, entire of itself; every man is a piece of the continent." Today, put into practice the words of the commercial used by the telephone company—"Reach out. Reach out and touch someone." Surround yourself with quality people and begin to encourage all the rest.

The law of attraction says that like attracts like. Perhaps in the past you have carried some baggage that attracted certain people, but now you are making important decisions to change, to become new in many ways. This law will continue to work, and you need to be ready to add a great new circle of friends who love the person you are becoming.

On your climb, surround yourself with those whose steps are certain. It's the safest way to reach the summit.

bend without breaking

Have you ever been on a jumbo jet when it headed into a violent storm? "Are we going to make it?" you may have wondered. The engineers who designed the aircraft thought a lot about such turbulence and designed the plane so it actually bends in flight with the forces of nature. The next time you're in a storm, look at the wings. You can actually see them flexing and yielding to the wind.

What about you? How do you respond in the midst of turmoil? How do you behave when suddenly confronted by a force that seems stronger than your own? Unfortunately, when most people are faced with a major problem, they respond by becoming extremely tense and inflexible. They clench their fists, set their jaw, and dare anyone to come within ten feet.

If your reactions are rigid, there is a much better approach. Use this hour to discover it. If, on the other hand, you are a person who practices the fine art of being adaptable and elastic in tough situations, use this hour to reinforce your ability to ride out the storms of life and even allow them to work for you.

Adaptability

Developing the ability to adapt quickly to difficult situations can pay large dividends. A Carnegie Foundation study showed that only 15 percent of a businessperson's success can be attributed to job knowledge and technical skills. These are essential elements but make a small overall contribution. What is most important? The research indicated that approximately 85 percent of one's success is determined by "attitude" and the "ability to deal with people." This requires immense flexibility.

People who rise to the top of their professions generally have developed an exceptional mastery of human relations. High on the list of their skills is the ability to be amiable and adaptable.

Being a successful boss, for example, requires flexibility. Fred Bucy, past president of Texas Instruments said,

> It doesn't take much talent to issue orders. It does take continued discipline to study the variety of people you are leading in order to understand what it takes to motivate them—and to inspire them to do their very best to make the company and themselves a success. It is a never-ending task to be an effective leader, because time changes all things. What might work at one point in time will not work at another point in time.[1]

Sticking to the old ways of doing things no longer works. Pick up any issue of a high-tech magazine and you'll get the message instantly. Research and development are making yesterday's products and methods outmoded before sunset. Just as we adapt to new discoveries, it is vital that we apply the same flexibility when dealing with people and procedures. Learn to bend quickly and adapt with speed.

There is an area, however, in which you should remain as sturdy as the Rock of Gibraltar. You should never compromise on personal standards or principles. There's a great difference between flexible decision making and practicing situational ethics.

Donald Kendall, chairman of PepsiCo says, "There's only one standard. Once you're stuck on the flypaper, you're stuck. If you don't set a high standard, you can't expect your people to act right."

Today, many companies are beginning to give ethics the highest possible priority. The Raytheon Company, for example, has a director of ethics compliance. All wrongdoings, difficult personnel issues, and ethical quandaries are reported to this person.

The Art of Attracting People

Being an effective leader requires the same skills, whether it is in a business, a school, a social club, a church, or even at home. Before people can be won to your ideas, *they must be won to you.*

The most powerful concepts in the world can be tossed aside if they are not presented by people who love people. Scripture records that Christ had more than a message from God. He also had such a warm personality that even little children gathered around him.

What is your personal strategy in attracting people to your point of view? Is it a stern, "Do this or else"? Or have you learned the fine art of leading people to a desired destination?

The key to winning friends and influencing people is to avoid making yourself a fountain of truth or a figure of unquestioned authority. Instead, show that you are a flexible, down-to-earth individual with a genuine interest in others.

Start Where They Are

Thomas Aquinas, the great medieval philosopher, was a master of education and persuasion. He taught that when you want to convert someone to your view, you walk over to where the person is standing, take him by the hand (mentally speaking), and guide him. Aquinas meant that you don't stand across the room and shout at him; you don't call him a "dummy," and you don't order him to come over to where you are. You start where he is and begin working from that position. Who must be flexible? *You!* It begins when you do the walking. This principle works whether you are leading, teaching, or negotiating.

Mark McCormack in his insightful book, *What They Don't Teach You at Harvard Business School*, explains how to make "bargaining" a win-win for both sides.

> I find it helpful to try to figure out in advance where the other person would like to end up—at what point he will do the deal and still feel like he's coming away with something. This is different from "How far will he go?" ... A lot of times you can push someone to the wall, and you still reach an agreement, but his resentment will come back to haunt you in a million ways.[2]

Your goal should be to negotiate so there are no bad feelings. And that requires flexibility.

Here's how a father used the principle on his son. About nine o'clock one evening he told his four-year-old boy, "I want you to pick up your toys before you go to bed." But it didn't work.

"I'm too tired," was the child's excuse.

Instead of becoming a dictator, the dad got down on the floor, lifted his son on his knees and said, "Humpty Dumpty sat on a wall. Humpty Dumpty had a great fall." And the boy fell.

"Let's do it again, Daddy."

So they did it again and again and again.

When the dad was about to quit, the little boy said, "Just one more time!"

"Not until you pick up your toys."

Without thinking, the child did in ninety seconds a job that could have taken him an hour.

When he jumped back on his father's knees, the dad said, "I thought you were too tired to pick up your toys."

"I was," said his son. "But I just wanted to do this."

"We" Is the Most Important Word

When people fail to respond to your suggestions and commands, don't become unpleasant. Instead, be flexible. Try a positive, creative approach, and you'll be surprised at the results.

The legendary football coach of the University of Alabama, Paul "Bear" Bryant, was asked what it takes to put together a championship football squad.

> I'm just a plowhand from Arkansas, but I have learned how to hold a team together. How to lift some men up, how to calm others down, until finally they've got one heartbeat together—a team. There's just three things I would tell them:
> "If anything goes bad, I did it.
> If anything goes semi-good, then we did it.
> If anything goes real good, then *you* did it."
> That's all it takes to get people to win football games for you.

Bryant knew that the word *you* is a word of empowerment.

A sign posted on the employee bulletin board of an Atlanta department store said,

> The six most important words in the English language are: "I admit I made a mistake."

The five most important words: "You did a great job."
The four most important words: "What is your opinion?"
The three most important words: "If you please."
The two most important words: "Thank you."
The single most important word: "We."
The least important word: "I."

If someone had to describe how you deal with others, what would they say? Would you be described as a commanding and stern taskmaster? Or as one who loves people and knows how to bring out the best in them?

Make an honest appraisal of your ability to adapt quickly to new situations. Brittle steel will shatter. When it has been tempered, however, it has been known to withstand a mighty earthquake.

Make a personal pact with yourself: "In every situation, I resolve to seek agreement rather than discord, to be responsive rather than use resistance, and to compromise rather than seek conflict." By putting those goals into practice, you can know what it means to "bend without breaking" and to "love without losing."

The power of positive thinking is great. But the strength of *flexibility thinking* can pay even greater dividends.

say farewell to unhealthy fear

Dealing with anxiety and worry has become a billion-dollar industry in America. We install sophisticated electronic security devices to protect our homes, visit medical clinics to check our immune systems, attend self-help seminars, see therapists, and buy extra flight insurance, just in case.

We live in a world where many have become paralyzed by fear. It is difficult to open the pages of *USA Today* without reading about people who are attempting to cope with insecurity.

Children cling to their parents because they are afraid of the dark. Men fear cutthroat competition or being out of a job. Women are frightened to walk down a city street because of the terror of rape. Fear is not something new. The words "fear not" appear in Scripture 365 times. That's once for every day of the year, but more important, it is God's message to you.

To become nervous in a new environment is natural; but if tension and anxiety have become part of your lifestyle and daily routine, you have reason for concern. Medical science has established that a prolonged state of fear and worry so affects the body that it sets the stage for almost every type of disease. It ravages the body's glandular and chemical balance and opens the floodgates to a sea of physical problems.

Many people are paralyzed by fear and worry. One man told his counselor, "If I don't worry enough, good things won't happen." He may deserve an "Anxiety Award," but his worry accomplishes nothing. It won't lead to a better job or make his life more productive. Worry is a cognitive distortion—a false expectation based on over-anticipating the worst that can happen. For many, it has become a part of their daily thought process.

Is it possible for a person who lives with constant worry and distress to experience a turn-around? Can someone who is filled with fright or plagued by phobias know full relaxation and security? Absolutely. It has happened to millions.

Motivated by Fear or Desire

Some people have a unique view of fear. They actually believe if they concentrate on what might go wrong, it will keep bad things from happening. But that's not the way it works. Worry is a monumental waste of time that saps your strength and postpones your pleasure.

Have you ever stopped to count how many of the things you worry about have actually come to pass? For most people, the number is small. It would be even smaller, however, if they had decided to avoid concentrating on the problem.

Most psychologists describe unhealthy fear or anxiety as a "cognitive distortion." That is a polite way of saying, "It's all in your head." Healthy fear, on the other hand, can serve a positive purpose and can even save your life. It is important to know the difference.

You may ask, "What is the basic cause of anxiety?" In many cases, it is the result of denying the reality of the present. Instead of dealing with a current truth, we leap ahead to a negative conclusion. Our thoughts can become so engrossed in what *might* happen that we begin to experience a physical and emotional response. People often describe feelings of anger, resentment, and hostility about events that *never* occur. The opposite is also true. We have the potential to be overcome by tears of joy and love just by yearning for a special person.

Both fear and desire are primary motivating forces. Fear is anticipation of punishment or pain, while desire is anticipation of reward. At various times we all move toward one or the other, and these feelings precede whatever eventually happens.

People say, "If I could just get motivated!" The truth is that they are *already* motivated by something. But is it the right thing? Of all negative drives, fear is often described as the most powerful. It restricts, inhibits, and causes feelings of uneasiness or apprehension. It also works to destroy your faith and vitality. Desire, however, is just the opposite. It is like a strong, positive magnet that attracts, reaches, opens, directs, and encourages.

It's pretty simple to know what force is in control. Every person is heavily influenced by his or her current dominant thoughts and perceptions, whether they are positive or negative.

Here is what happened to the great Milwaukee baseball pitcher Warren Spahn. He was on the mound pitching to Nelson Howard, the New York Yankee slugger. The score was tied 2 to 2 in the ninth inning. There were two outs and two men on base. The catcher walked out to Spahn and said, "Don't throw him a high outsider."

That was the wrong thing to say. His words were like a flashing neon sign that had suddenly been turned on. Spahn wound up and delivered exactly what the catcher had branded on his brain.

It was a high outsider, so high that it sailed into the stands and the Yankees won the game.

It was like someone telling you, "For the next sixty seconds, don't think about a flying elephant." The idea, once planted, is impossible to avoid. Even if you dwell on the reverse of an idea, you will be controlled by it.

Many people believe that they can resolve a dilemma by trying to escape it. But they become bound by the very things they wrestle. The more they struggle, the more they are ensnared.

Psychologist Scott Peck makes a strong statement: "The tendency to avoid problems and the emotional suffering inherent in them is the primary basis of all mental illness."[1] It is our attempt to *avoid* the problem that leads us to great difficulty.

You may say, "It sounds hopeless! If I concentrate on my problems I'm in trouble, and if I try *not* thinking about my fears I get the same result. What is the answer?"

A New Perspective

Erasing the word *fearful* from your self-evaluation begins with a decision to *take control of your dominating thoughts*. Positive people aren't always born that way. Most of them have experienced enough pain and agony for a lifetime and have decided they no longer want to live that way. *Deliberately fix your thoughts on healthy outcomes.* Choose a scenario of hope and expectation and stay with that thought until you can visualize the positive outcome. Hostages in the Middle East who spent years in dark, dismal prisons survived by replacing thoughts of their dire circumstances with creative dreams. Terry Anderson reported spending months mentally designing a complete dairy farm down to the last tiny detail. He also read the Bible more than fifty times. These activities became his means of hope and life.

Next, instead of staring at your problem, get a new perspective. First-grade children, when asked to draw a picture of their mother or father, are likely to draw stick figures with long, long legs and tiny heads. Why? Because that is how they see an adult. From their vantage point, the parent's legs look mighty long.

The skyline of New York City is impressive, but when you walk the streets what you see is often not a pretty sight. If you want a totally different picture of Manhattan, however, you can take an elevator to the top of the Empire State Building. From that view, the street-level problems seem to shrink, and you see the city from a different perspective.

When you stand next to the pressures you face, they can seem overwhelming; but when you view them from a higher perspective— seeing them in light of the resources, including prayer, available to you—the problems seem smaller.

Your next step is to expand your creativity. In the business world, executives rise to the top by demonstrating their originality and imagination. One computer company promotes its product creativeness by asking the question, "What if?" For example, "What if we rearranged the keyboard so it could be used with three or four fingers of just one hand?" Or, "What if the computer commands could be triggered by a verbal command of 'yes' or 'no'?"

If you continue to think about your problems in the same old way, you'll be digging a hole that will someday be so deep you can't escape. Instead of taking a shovel and moving dirt, start looking for answers in new locations. You'll be surprised at the mental power you can unlock by looking for "What if?" solutions.

Take a Risk!

Instead of trying to eliminate fear, try accepting it as appropriate when you're stepping into something new. "Hold on," you say, "that sounds like a dangerous path." What many people fail to realize is that *everyone* experiences anxiety. Even self-confident actors find their knees shaking on opening night. A head of a Fortune 500 company may break out in a cold sweat if he is interviewed on *60 Minutes*.

There is nothing wrong with admitting that you are fearful of a new situation. It would be abnormal if you *didn't* feel apprehension. In fact, acknowledging the fear gives you power over it.

What is the best way to manage your fear of the future? Replace it with a concern for the present. In other words: Take a risk!

In her book *Feel the Fear and Do It Anyway*, Dr. Susan Jeffers says,

> As long as I continue to push out into the world, as long as I continue to stretch my capabilities, as long as I continue to take risks in making my dreams come true, I am going to experience fear.[2]

Most of us grow up waiting for fear to go away, but the best way to eliminate fear is to face it. With every new challenge comes anxiety. That's a sign of normal growth and development. Dr. David Viscott says, "Not risking is the surest way of losing. If you do not risk, risk eventually comes to you."[3] Why wait for circumstances to control your life? Accept the challenge in every situation, even if it involves taking a chance, and learn to accept the fear as a positive thing.

Replace Fear with Faith

The plight of Job is summed up in his words, "The thing I greatly feared has come upon me" (Job 3:25). Jesus, however, had a new vocabulary. He said, "According to your faith be it unto you." And to a woman who was sick, 'Thy faith has made you whole."

Why anxiously wait for a solution? Do what you can do and disengage yourself from the outcome. Trust God and his promises.

Have faith. Relax. You don't plant a seed and dig it up. Let it take root and grow. A doctor can't heal a cut on your arm. He can just rearrange the tissue and allow the healing to begin.

Instead of allowing fear to cripple your future, decide that you will face it head-on and use it as a force to propel you. All ducks have wings, but many can't fly because they've been paddling in the water too long. Many adults are like children who pretend they are swimming when they are actually walking on the bottom of the pool.

Saying farewell to unhealthy fears is not a slow, painful process that takes a generation. It can happen today if you decide to control the events and thoughts that are pointing you in the wrong direction. Get a new perspective, take a risk, and begin to act with faith.

You'll be able to say hello to healthy fears and kiss your unhealthy ones good-bye.

winning by quitting

"How am I ever going to break that habit?" Millions of people think about such a question every day.

An accountant in Atlanta says, "That's the last cigarette I'm ever going to smoke!" Then, thirty minutes later he is puffing a Marlboro and wondering how it could have reached his lips.

A lady in Los Angeles has tried a hundred known diets and invented one or two of her own. Her compulsion to overeat, however, leaves her totally powerless. "Why did I do that?" she ponders after swallowing the last morsel of a candy bar.

Our media is filled with the appalling stories of people who seem helpless to control their deep-seated urge for alcohol, mind-controlling drugs, abusive behavior, gambling, and a horrid host of self-destructive acts. Countless people are enslaved by an overwhelming addiction.

But what about a minor habit? How do you react when you see people biting their nails, continually scratching their head, cracking their knuckles, or saying "you know" five times every minute? Those are compulsive behaviors too, and if not checked they can grow to become major distractions in life. As Horace Mann wrote, "Habit is a cable; we weave a thread of it every day, and at last we cannot break it."[1]

Health experts believe that many people could live twice as long if they didn't spend the first half of their lives acquiring habits that shorten the other half. Jacquelyn Small says that addiction, which is a strong habit, "is a way of staying stuck in the past, repeating like a robot the same worn out modes of operation that do not work."[2]

As you inventory your personal behavior list, there are likely to be items you want to change. Where should you begin? Can you toss all of your habits overboard at once? No. That's not the way it works. You have to deal with them one at a time.

Breaking Old Habits

Not all personal patterns are negative. The person who says, "If I could only break my habits, I'd be a success!" fails to realize that habits are vital to our daily existence. Without them, we'd be hopelessly lost.

When you were three or four years old, someone taught you how to tie your shoes. It would be sad if you had to relearn that lesson every day for the rest of your life. Fortunately, it has become a habitual routine, like brushing your teeth or combing your hair.

In our formative years we acquire personal habits that serve us for a lifetime. We can take comfort in the fact that the good usually far outnumber the bad. In virtually all cases, we pattern our lives after our parents and remain mirrors of them until we become young adults.

Research by Lionel Standing and Bruce Nicholson on student drinking and smoking reported in *Social Behavior and Personality* indicates that the behavior of university students corresponds to the behavior of their parents, from childhood through the first two years of campus life. At that point a shift takes place in their actions, and they become strongly influenced by their friends.[3]

While most of what we pattern is positive, just one addictive behavior can become like a virus that invades our entire system and causes an imbalance in our ability to function.

You will never know success in breaking a habit if you concentrate on the behavior. That only reinforces it. Most of our failure to rid ourselves of bad habits can be compared to what has been called the "Wallenda factor." You may recall the famous circus tightrope walker, Karl Wallenda, who was killed years ago in a tragic fall. His widow was quoted as saying, "All Karl thought about for three straight months prior to the accident was falling. It seemed to me that he put all his energy into *not* falling—rather than into walking the tightrope."

Kicking the habit will not come by focusing on the unwanted behavior, but by a clear picture of a positive alternative. For example, you are less likely to break the smoking habit by seeing a cigarette trampled under your foot than by seeing yourself breathing clean, healthy air. This way you are focusing on the beneficial outcome.

Winning by quitting does not need to be a long, painful process. Far more people have permanently abandoned compulsive behavior because they made a decision based on a personal desire to grow, than by expensive treatments or extended years of counseling.

What is it that they decide? To replace an undesired behavior with a healthy one. That's right! They become *addicted*, but to a new daily activity that is positive.

Good Habits Can Lead to Success

A young man worked his way through college selling encyclopedias. Here's how he used the power of habit to become a success.

"Every day I would work from a list of one hundred phone numbers to set up appointments," he said. "After twelve people agreed to see my demonstration, I would pick out the six that sounded the most promising. Three would let me in the door, and I would average one sale each night."

He was asked, "Well, did you go back and call on the other good prospects?'

He said, "Oh, no! The next day I started with a fresh list of one hundred numbers and did it all over again."

He played the odds and it worked day after day. It taught him discipline and self-reliance. But most important, he learned that establishing a daily habit can lead to success.

William H. Danforth, who became the wealthy owner of the Ralston Purina Company in St. Louis, found the secret of success when he was young. At the age of sixteen he knew what he wanted. He told his biographer that he discovered the secret in a rather curious way.

> When I was sixteen, I came to St. Louis to attend the Manual Training School. It was a mile from my boardinghouse to the school. A teacher who lived nearby and I would start for school at the same time every morning. But he always beat me there. Even back then I didn't want to be beaten, and so I tried all the shortcuts. Day after day, however, he arrived ahead of me. Then I discovered how he did it. When he came to each street crossing he would run to the other curb. The thing that put him ahead of me was just "that little extra."[4]

Most people wouldn't consider such a small action important. Danforth applied his newfound habit of extra effort to every area of his professional life.

The "Decision" Habit

Instead of shining your spotlight on habits you want to break, try creating a list of behaviors you want to *add*. Here's an example.

Determine to acquire the habit of making quick decisions. Perhaps you have known some people you regard as lucky for the simple reason that they can decide everything in a flash—and are usually right. A proposal comes to them. It involves two, three, or even a half-dozen options. Do they hesitate? Not a bit. They decide instantly, then go quickly on to the next item. This is the pattern they continue throughout the day.

Are these instant deciders just born that way? A few may be, but usually this ability to decide instantly and correctly is the result of acquired habit.

Psychologists Donald and Eleanor Laird believe that it is easy to acquire this pattern. They say it's a matter of following a simple formula. When you need to decide on a specific thing, write down a few questions.

Will it make it work easier?

Will it add to your safety and success?

What else will it do?

Then, with the questions before you, decide whether the matter will give you positive or negative answers. If positive, the answer is easy, "yes." If negative, it is equally easy, "no."[5]

This habit of simple analysis based on a few questions will give you the skill you need to develop one of the most priceless of all success skills—that of making executive decisions.

In time you will be able to dispense with the written questions. You will raise them in your mind and answer them without the formal process of putting them down on paper. But in the beginning, until the habit becomes firmly fixed, write first and then answer.

That's just one of thousands of ways in which you can form building blocks of success by deliberately forming positive habits in every area of your life—personal, business, social, and spiritual.

What's Happening Inside?

The cure for bad habits begins with internal transformation rather than external reformation. When you are happy with *you*, a multitude of satisfying things begin to happen. Psychologists tell us that the physical condition of our bodies is often a reflection of our inner mental and emotional health. As a sign in an agricultural supply store said, "If you don't like the crop you're reaping, check the seed you are sowing." Thoughts of love and self-acceptance serve as seeds for healthy physical well-being.

Your decision should not be to see how many destructive patterns you can break, but rather how many positive habits you can establish. Dr. William Lee Wilbanks, a lecturer on willpower and a professor of criminal justice at Florida International University, says, "We are not simply animals ruled by instincts and impulses. We can control our own behavior if we believe we can." Like taking a morning shower, make positive thoughts a daily practice. The words of the apostle Paul need repeating: "Finally, brethren, whatever things are true, whatever things are noble, whatever things are just, whatever things are pure, whatever things are lovely, whatever things are of good report, if there is any virtue and if there is anything praiseworthy—meditate on these things" (Phil. 4:8).

What habit will you break today? What habit will you make?

take charge of your emotions

Emotions, whether we like them or not, are an inescapable part of our lives. Feelings of desire, anger, fear, courage, envy, pity, regret, hatred, love, and joy are not reserved for Oscar-winning actors, children, and television. We all experience them. Long ago, Aristotle defined emotion as simply "whatever is attended by pleasure or pain."

The word *emotion* comes from the Latin term that means "to move." Our emotions are constantly steering us toward or away from something. In many cases, they motivate us appropriately to deal with our surroundings, whether hostile or friendly.

Good Servants but Bad Masters

It would be a utopian world if we felt only sensations of love, joy, and peace. But we must also deal with emotions that are, by their very nature, destructive. For some it becomes a cycle of chaos. As the Scottish philosopher David Hume wrote, "Grief and disappointment give rise to anger, anger to envy, envy to malice, and malice to grief again, till the whole circle is completed."

Physicians have long known that emotional disorder usually precedes physical disorder. It's not only the germ that causes the disease; it's a weakened immune system that allows the germ to invade the body. When your emotions are vulnerable, your systems are defenseless. Disease is like water pouring through a ruptured dam.

If negative feelings such as discouragement, despondency, and fear linger long enough, the psyche becomes the controlling force and the body responds accordingly. As Roger L'Estrange wrote, "It is with our passions as it is with fire and water—they are good servants but bad masters."

Our Basic Needs

The noted psychologist Abraham Maslow viewed our behavior as a response to "Five Basic Needs." He organized them in a range from lower to higher. He said that we can't be free to satisfy our higher needs until our lower needs are met.

1. *Physiological needs*—food, water, air
2. *Safety needs*—freedom from threat of danger, need to be around the familiar and secure
3. *"Belongingness" and love needs*—affiliation, acceptance
4. *Esteem needs*—achievement, strength, competition, reputation, status, prestige
5. *Need for self-actualization*—self-fulfillment, the realization of potentialities

Most people rise above steps one and two, but never reach fulfillment in step five. Why? They become bogged down dealing with the emotional issues surrounding their need for love and self-esteem, steps three and four.

It is important to recognize emotions for what they are—God-given feelings that allow us to experience life to its fullest. We all come into the world with sensitivity and awareness, but in our desire to seek approval we learn to repress our feelings. We all do our best to restrain and control what is not acceptable. We need to recognize that there is nothing wrong with experiencing a wide range of emotions. That should be our goal. Many adults, however, have never released some of the destructive emotions of their childhood, and this inhibits their experiencing a range of emotions as adults. Those who teach on the subject of "inner healing" know the importance of liberating repressed feelings. When we look back at a past occurrence and attach new meaning to it, restoration begins.

Sometimes, to liberate the feeling we must examine the painful experience that caused us to repress the emotion. How can the pain be erased? It usually involves a three-step process:

1. We *revisit* the emotion or incident.
2. We *relive* that memory with God's guidance in the present.
3. The conscious mind *reviews* the buried memory with new awareness of the truth, which defuses its power to hurt us.

Recovery will occur when we cease trying to avoid or repress negative emotional experiences. As Carl Jung said, "A man who has not passed through the inferno of his passions has never overcome them."

Who Is Responsible?

It is important to remember that we are responsible for our own actions and reactions.

For many, the most destructive emotion in their lives is the four-letter word *hate*. It seems that the mere thought of a particular person can cause negative passions to rise. The question we need to ask is, "Who is really the source of the problem?" The German poet Herman Hesse spoke directly to the issue when he said, "If you hate a person, you hate something in him that is part of yourself. What isn't part of ourselves doesn't disturb us." We have a tendency to react negatively to the dark shadows in others that also reside in ourselves.

Have you ever heard someone say, "I can't stand to be around her—she makes me so unhappy"? Whether we realize it or not, what others say and do to us can only affect us if we allow it to. It's what is within us that truly affects us. Jesus taught that it is not what goes into a person that defiles him or her but what comes out of the heart that defiles the person (Mark 7:18–23).

We will never be released from emotions such as hatred or jealousy until we realize that other people are not responsible for our happiness. They also are not responsible for our *unhappiness*. The response to relationships shattered by these emotions must be to personally accept the responsibility for our feelings. Excuses such as, "It's their fault," or, "If it were not for . . ." need to be discarded as resistance to personal responsibility.

Our dealings with people present a never-ending stream of emotional responses. Psychiatrist David Viscott, in *The Language of Feelings*, says that each time two people meet, there is an immediate sense of warmth or coldness, of power or vulnerability. "Everybody has felt threatened at some point by the mere presence of a menacing person, even when he says nothing. . . . The change you perceive is the emotional 'aura' of the other person. It varies and changes in a person just as his feelings do."[1]

In recent years biological research has led to the discovery of endorphins. Dr. Candace Pert, one of the pioneers of this discovery, describes endorphins: "These are chemicals produced by the body that become painkillers more powerful than any opiate known; they also can have a regenerating effect on the human body." How are they released? Dozens of ways, including through the simple act of a pat on the back, a warm hug, or a smile.

As humans, we need meaningful encounters of love and acceptance that release these chemicals so important to our well-being. We all have the capacity for relating well to others, for self-awareness, self-acceptance, personal development, autonomy, and deep personal experiences. It takes effort, however, to develop these areas.

Human beings are a unique creation of God and our ability to form an identity and then attach value to it distinguishes us from the rest of creation. God gives us the capacity to define who we are and then allows us to decide if we like ourselves.

We can be repulsed by certain sounds, colors, or images, but when we refuse to accept ourselves, we are then unable to develop the capacities within us that God designed to allow us to function well. We should never forget that the Bible says, "the kingdom of God is within you" (Luke 17:21). Because Christ dwells within us, we have the ability to see ourselves as God sees us and to attach his value to ourselves. We "have put on the new man who is renewed in knowledge according to the image of Him who created him" (Col. 3:10).

From the Heart

What a beautiful world it is when your heart gets involved. The great composer Igor Stravinsky said, "I haven't understood a bar of music in my life, but I have felt it."

In education, a clear distinction is made between thinking and feeling. The cognitive domain involves the mind. What do we mean? How do we comprehend? How do we analyze it? How do we apply it? But there is another world known as the affective domain that involves the heart. How do you feel about it? What about your emotions? What have you experienced? G. K. Chesterton put it this way, "There is a road from the eye to the heart that does not go through the intellect."

Your life won't experience meaningful change if your commitment stops at the cognitive level. In that case, the only benefit will be your ability to explain the basics to someone else. Instead of getting caught up in the age of "cosmetic surgery," we need to make our decisions based on the fact that it is what's on the inside that counts. George Bernard Shaw was talking about more than the surface when he said, "Better keep yourself clean and bright; you are the window through which you must see the world."

You may have heard the statement, "As a man thinketh, so is he." But that's not how it goes. You need to add the three missing words. "For as he thinks in his heart, so is he" (Prov. 23:7). Where? *In his heart!* Even your speech is a reflection of the real you. "For out of the abundance of the heart the mouth speaks" (Matt. 12:34).

Simply trying to think good thoughts and speak clever words won't produce a turn-around. Your true character is what is on the inside.

Taking Charge

For more than twenty years, there was a "dark side" to Fred Briggs's behavior. Those who didn't know him well would say he was an affable, hardworking family man who had few vices. He didn't drink or smoke. But to close friends and family, he was a different story.

What was Fred's problem? The smallest irritation would cause his temper to rage out of control. "It seemed I was powerless to contain my anger. Suddenly, I would lash out with a torrent of loud profanity that I could not repress."

It usually happened at home, but more and more, his outbursts would occur at the office or wherever else something happened he didn't particularly like.

At the age of twenty-eight, with a wife and two small children, he realized that his temper tantrums were going to leave an indelible imprint on his family and might even cost him his job. Fred decided to do something about it.

"One morning, I got up early, looked at myself in the mirror, and said, 'Fred. You are never, never, ever again going to lose your temper. *Never!*'"

Most people would laugh at the possibility that such a simple declaration could drastically alter a deep-rooted behavior. There was one difference, however, between Fred's decision and those of most people. Fred's commitment came from the heart, and he meant every word of it.

"It was like a drug addict going 'cold turkey,'" he said. "The moment I felt the first signal of impending anger, I would recognize it and remember my vow. In fact, I looked forward to those feelings just to prove again and again that I was in control of my actions."

Later, his wife actually *tried* to provoke his temper to see if his transformation was real. "I can smile about it now," he said, "because I'm a totally changed man."

Fred, unlike most of us, took control of his emotions in one great moment of decision.

Fred Briggs was able to take charge of his outbursts of anger because he *decided* to. It didn't take a decade or even a day. It happened instantly—and permanently—because the commitment came from the source of his strongest emotion. It came from his heart.

Don't delay in making an inventory of the emotions that continue to negatively affect you. Choose the one that is causing the most harm and make the decision for permanent change.

revolutionize your data bank

Some teens in Denver were asked, "What are your plans for the future?"

"To learn a skill and get a job," was the first reply. Most of the answers, in one form or another, were similar.

You can travel to Africa or Asia and hear the same response. Will their objectives be met? Many of them will. But what will happen in the years that follow? For most people, the moment they enter the workforce, the educational process will end, and their personal growth will be minimal.

Successful leaders, on the other hand, are those whose data banks never stop expanding. Their minds are like giant computers, with new memory chips being added to hold the material. To them, new concepts and fresh information are as important as the air they breathe.

The great motivator, Charles "Tremendous" Jones, said, "You are the same today that you are going to be five years from now except for two things: the people with whom you associate, and the books you read."[1] It's important, then, to consider which people and which books will influence and change you. What kind of input should you be receiving? What voices should you be hearing? What printed matter should you be spending time with? And how can you apply the new information to achieve the greatest results?

Developing a personal continuing-education program needs to become an item of high priority. It also involves commitment to a specific plan of action. Here are three recommendations:

1. Spend a few minutes every day exploring a topic that is brand-new to you.
2. Deliberately ask questions designed to obtain fresh and innovative information.
3. Read or listen to at least ten minutes of self-help, motivational material every day.

Out of the Ordinary

Why should you take the time to absorb data in an area that is foreign to you? That's the essence of a liberal arts education. It expands your horizons and gives you the ability to communicate with people at a level you never imagined.

You may want to go beyond the level of reading and actually *experience* it.

Jessamyn West, in her book *To See the Dream*, said,

If I were to join a circle of any kind, it would be a circle that required its members to try something new at least once a month.

The new thing could be very inconsequential: steak for breakfast, frog hunting, walking on stilts, memorizing a stanza of poetry. It could be staying up outdoors all night, making up a dance and dancing it, speaking to a stranger, chinning yourself, milking a goat, reading the Bible—anything not ordinarily done.[2]

Adding variety and adventure to your lifestyle is exciting. And, as an added benefit, you'll be surprised at your ability to recall the details of your experience or information at the right time.

Author C. D. Board says,

Each person is at each moment capable of remembering all that has ever happened to him. The function of the brain and nervous system is to protect us from being overwhelmed and confused by the mass of largely useless and irrelevant knowledge, by shooting out most of what we should otherwise perceive or remember at any moment, and leaving only that very small and special selection which is likely to be practically useful.[3]

Don't worry about having an information overload. Your objective of lifelong learning should be to seek knowledge wherever it can be found.

Being an expert in a particular field is desirable, but often it is the ability to link a variety of topics together that becomes important. In his book, *The Structure of Scientific Revolutions*, T. S. Kuhn tells us that many significant discoveries have been made by young scientists or people entering into a field of study where they were not "brainwashed" by accepted theory. The fact that Einstein was a high school dropout did not limit his ability.

On your next visit to the public library, try checking out books you never before considered reading. Sacheverell Sitwell, who wrote *Monks, Nuns, and Monasteries*, was consumed with the topic. Perhaps you will be too. Before long you may find yourself reading everything from *The Art of Hang Gliding* to *The Life and Times of William Jennings Bryan*.

Intentional Listening

When Lyndon B. Johnson was a junior senator from Texas, he kept a sign on his office wall that read, "You ain't learnin' nothin' when you're doin' all the talkin.'"

It is important to develop the habit of intentional listening. The best way for that to happen is to start asking questions—plenty of them. And then listen to the answers.

Sam Walton, founder of Wal-Mart who became one of the richest men in America, believed in hearing what people—especially his employees—had to say. Once he flew his aircraft to Mt. Pleasant, Texas, and parked the plane with instructions to his copilot to meet him one hundred or so miles down the road. He then flagged a Wal-Mart truck and rode the rest of the way to "chat with the driver." He said, "It seemed like so much fun." It was also a great learning experience.

Dallas-based Chili's, one of the nation's five best-run food service chains, according to *Restaurants & Institutions* magazine, is another company with a leader who listens to employees. Norman Brinker, Chili's chairman, believes that responsive communication is the key to good relations with both employees and customers. He also has learned that such communication pays big dividends. Almost 80 percent of Chili's menu came from suggestions made by unit managers.

Many people go through the routine of listening, but they're hearing the wrong message. It's like the two men who were walking along the streets of London when music from a nearby cathedral came floating by. One of the men remarked, "Isn't that wonderful music?"

"I didn't hear what you said," the other man replied.

"Aren't those chimes beautiful?" repeated the first speaker. But again the other man was unable to catch the words, and the first speaker said for the third time, "Isn't that lovely music?"

"It's no use," came the answer. "Those pesky bells are making so much noise I can't hear a word you're saying."

An accountant figured out how much a company loses because people are not listening. He said, "The typical employee spends about three-quarters of every working day in verbal communication. Nearly half of that is spent listening. If it is true that the average employee is about 25 percent effective as a listener, it means that if a manager receives a salary of $50,000 per year, over $12,500 of it is paid for being an ineffective listener."

Focus your attention on what others have to say and ask specific questions designed to get people talking. It is a well-known fact that knowledge is power, and you can't receive it if you are dispensing all of the information. Start listening.

An Atmosphere of Optimism

Among the world's all-time bestselling books are volumes of personal inspiration, including Dale Carnegie's *How to Win Friends and Influence People* and Napoleon Hill's *Think and Grow Rich*.

Many people may read such books in their formative years, and that's the end of it. For some reason, they never again feel the need to read motivational material.

In 1972, Ken Lipke founded Gibraltar Steel Company in Buffalo, New York, with a personal investment of $500. Twenty years later he was a multimillionaire with an extremely profitable corporation in one of the world's toughest businesses. How did it happen? Lipke said,

I knew practically nothing about the steel business when I began. As a young man, I was trained to be a chiropractor. But one of my early mentors turned me on to self-help reading, and I realized that having a great vision and developing the ability to lead people would be my greatest asset. I never stopped reading inspirational books and applying the principles to my business.[4]

Lipke learned that finding people with technical skills and detailed knowledge of steel processing was easy. Qualified accountants, managers, and salespeople were abundant. But the ideas he learned from people like Robert Schuller and Norman Vincent Peale were his spark plugs. He developed the ability to build an atmosphere of optimism and teamwork that resulted in a giant corporation.

Allen H. Neuharth, founder of *USA Today*, said, "Don't just learn something from every experience; learn something positive."

We need to recognize the fact that nearly every "You can do it" book contains essentially the same message told in a variety of ways. Why is it important to develop a program to continue reading such material? As a corporate president in St. Louis said, "I have read *Think and Grow Rich* once each year for all of my adult life. Every time I read it, the volume seems brand-new to me. I continue to grow by applying the ideas to my life and work. The book may stay the same, but I am a brand-new person who is reading it."

Self-help volumes are unique because you don't have to start at chapter one to find inspiration. You can open such a book at almost any page and find advice worth applying. Here's a simple recommendation for a daily motivational reading program. Keep a book near your bed and read ten pages a day. If it is the sixth day of the month, start on page sixty. If it is the fourteenth day, start on page 140 and read ten pages.

It's equally important that you choose a concept to immediately put into practice. Only by fleshing out the principles will they come alive and become a permanent part of your behavior.

The most important book for personal growth is the Bible. It should become the cornerstone of your daily reading program.

Throughout history, great leaders have been great learners. Theodore Roosevelt died with a book under his pillow, consuming the ideas of others until the very last.

Never, never stop growing. Plateaus should only be found in geography books, not in personal experience. The key to a revolution in your mental data bank is to take in far more than you give out.

Read widely, listen carefully, and put self-help principles into action every day.

how to reorder your day

Horace Mann created an unforgettable "classified ad" when he wrote, "Lost: Somewhere between sunrise and sunset, two golden hours, each set with sixty diamond minutes. No reward is offered for they are gone forever."

What would happen if you were suddenly given some extra time every day, even sixty minutes? How would your life be changed? Many would use it to advance their careers. Others would use it for their hobbies, with friends, for reading, even for an extra hour's sleep.

It is important to know that while you cannot create time, you can effectively *control* it. By exercising power over the *use* of time, your day can be reordered in many profound ways.

Have you ever stopped to calculate the value of an hour? Ben Franklin did. One morning, he was busy preparing his newspaper for printing when a customer stopped in his store and spent an hour browsing the various books for sale. Finally, he took one in his hand and asked the shop assistant the cost.

The assistant answered, "One dollar."

The customer said, "A dollar. Can't you sell it for less?"

"No, the price is a dollar," replied the assistant.

The customer said he wanted to see Mr. Franklin. When Ben appeared from the back room, the customer asked how much he wanted for the book.

Franklin said, "One dollar and a quarter."

The customer was taken aback. "Your assistant asked for only a dollar."

Franklin said, "If you had bought it from him, I could sell it to you for a dollar. But you have taken me away from the business I was engaged in."

The customer pressed on, "Come on, Mr. Franklin, what is the lowest you can take for it?'

Franklin said, "One dollar and a half. And the longer we discuss it, the more of my time you are taking up and the more I'll have to charge you."

Time-Management Principles

Your moments are valuable too. By taking a new look at the ticks of the clock, you can allow time to work *for* you instead of against you. Here are ten specific things you can do.

Live in the Present

You can't rewrite history, although some people certainly try. Others daydream about what will happen tomorrow. But life is meant to be lived in the present. Only *now* are we capable of controlling our lives. It is important to have goals, but the future is determined by the conscious choices we make today. That is why it is vital that you become focused on the immediate time you have been granted.

Here's the advice given by the apostle Paul, "See then that you walk circumspectly, not as fools but as wise, redeeming the time" (Eph. 5:15–16).

Place a Value on Your Activity

Ben Franklin did it, and you can too. Every day you exchange one day of your life for the specific things you are doing. Is your activity worth it?

Many people who set their financial goals on an annual basis fail to calculate what they need to produce every day or every hour to achieve it. When you determine the value of just one minute of your working day, you will treat it with much greater respect.

Create a Written Daily Schedule

Since time is moving in an orderly manner, you must respond accordingly. Write down your daily activities, and don't stop with your nine-to-five work. What about your personal and family life? Have you set aside significant time for those you love? What about time for reading or physical exercise?

Many people talk about having a well-balanced life, but it is not reflected in their schedule. Success is much more than being in control of your business activities. Take the time to write a twenty-four-hour plan.

Prioritize Your Tasks

Most people begin a "Things to Do Today" list with the most pleasurable task as item one. Instead, tasks should be listed in order of difficulty. Schedule the most time-consuming and toughest task first. That's when you have the most energy. Then, as the tasks become shorter and more enjoyable, you'll sustain your energy by doing something you really like.

Make Effective Use of Short Periods of Time

It has been proven again and again that fifteen minutes a day devoted to one subject will make a person a master of it in five years. Instead of thinking in terms of days, or even hours, plan your schedule in terms of short periods of productive activity. Then, when someone is ten or fifteen minutes late for an appointment, your time isn't wasted. You have a plan for those moments.

Many people, for example, are overwhelmed at the thought of writing a book, but if they take a few minutes to write just a half page—about 150 words a day—they will have a manuscript of over 50,000 words in a year.

Don't Allow Others to Determine Your Schedule

In a cartoon in the *Wall Street Journal* a boss was speaking to an employee. "It's lonely at the top, Harris, but it's not so lonely that I want you walking into my office twenty times a day."

You must be in charge of your day. You must determine what time you'll devote to which activity and then be adamant about not allowing intrusions on that time. Don't allow a telephone call to interrupt your work. Set aside specific times of the day for placing or returning phone calls. Get in the habit of scheduling a series of short appointments, even ten or fifteen minutes apart, rather than at hourly intervals. This ensures that time isn't wasted with idle chatter. If you think in terms of an hour, that's how long your meetings will last. A talkative person will have to leave when the next appointment arrives.

Work Smart

Dale Carnegie told the story of two men who were out chopping wood. One man worked hard all day, took no breaks, and stopped only briefly for lunch. The other chopper took several breaks during the day and a short nap at lunch. At the end of the day, the woodman who had taken no breaks was quite disturbed to see that the other chopper had cut more wood than he had.

He said, "I don't understand. Every time I looked around, you were sitting down, yet you cut more wood than I did."

His companion replied, "Did you also notice that while I was sitting down I was sharpening my ax?"[1]

Recognize Time-Wasters

Businessman H. L. Hunt gave up smoking cigars many years ago, but it wasn't for reasons of health. It was the profit motive. The way he figured it, just the time he took to unwrap and light his cigars—time he otherwise could have spent concentrating on his work—was costing him several hundred dollars a year.

We need to recognize which activities waste our time. Those who have mastered the art of quick work know we can speed up our daily process. Many decisions, for example, can be made instantly. But we get in the habit of saying, "Let me think about it." Some people waste time by concentrating on issues that are irrelevant and unimportant.

Robert Frost wrote, "The brain is a wonderful organ; it starts working the moment you get up in the morning and does not stop until you get into the office." As someone bluntly put it, "The Lord gave you two ends—one for sitting and one for thinking. Your success depends on which you use. Heads you win, tails you lose."

Focus on Personal Productivity

The *Los Angeles Times* reported that James A. Fields, a noted management consultant, stated that the average worker is productive only 55 percent of the time. "About 15 percent of his effort is lost to 'personal time,' but 30 percent is lost through scheduling problems, unclear assignments, improper staffing and poor discipline."[2]

When Domino's Pizza, one of America's largest chains, announced that any customer would receive a $3 discount if it took longer than thirty minutes for the home delivery of a pizza, something amazing happened. It wasn't just the customer who benefited but also Domino's. Their entire national workforce put things into high gear, finding ways to save time. As a result, the productivity of the entire operation was moved ahead significantly.

Do It Now

Now is a three-letter word that can mean the difference between success and failure. It can give you instant motivation if you look at it positively.

There are dozens of ways to put a "now plan" to work every day. Here is one example. Every time a piece of paper comes to your attention, do one of three things with it immediately:

1. throw it away
2. take action on it
3. file it

You'll be amazed to see how organized your life can seem when this becomes a habit.

Thomas Huxley said, "Perhaps the most valuable result of all education is the ability to make yourself do the things you have to do, when they ought to be done, whether you like it or not." It is a lesson that needs to be learned.

The Value of One Minute

Begin by putting just one of these time-management principles into practice. Even if it saves one minute, the effort will be well spent.

A minute doesn't sound like much, but it has value beyond measure. Sixty seconds is all the time an advertiser has to tell people about a product. To an auto racer it means the difference between victory and defeat. To a surgeon it can mean the time between life or death.

Remember, tomorrow is nothing more than a series of todays. There isn't time to waste on idle dreams. Every minute counts. We need to be guided by the words a salesman printed on the back of his business card:

> I have only just a minute.
> Only sixty seconds in it.
> Didn't seek it, didn't choose it.
> But it's up to me to use it.
> I must suffer if I lose it.
> Give account if I abuse it.
> Just a tiny little minute.
> But eternity is in it.

making the most of your money

In this hour you will be asked to make a decision that can have a dramatic impact on your finances.

The desire to obtain wealth is nothing new. Centuries ago the Greeks told the story of Dionysius who asked King Midas what he wanted more than anything else on earth. Midas said, "My greatest wish in life is that everything I touch would turn into gold."

Dionysius granted Midas his wish. To test his new powers, Midas reached up and plucked a leaf from a tree. It turned to gold in his hand. Next he picked up a small pebble and it instantly turned into the precious metal.

Midas was ecstatic. He shouted for joy, "I am the richest man in the world." Then he added, "I am the *happiest* man in the world."

When he returned home, Midas asked his servants to prepare a feast. Soon he became thirsty. He drank some wine, but to everyone's amazement it turned to gold on his lips. He asked for some bread, but it also turned to gold before he took the first bite. When he reached out to touch his daughter, she too turned to gold.

Today, people still wish for the Midas touch, without considering what might happen if all their wishes really came true.

When we talk about money, it is important to separate myth from reality. You may ask if it's possible that just one decision about finances can drastically alter a person's economic future. Can an average individual with an ordinary income create wealth? Absolutely. It is happening every day, and in this hour we will show you how.

The Meaning of Money

Those who glibly say, "Money is not important," are not facing the facts. The average person spends more time earning the medium of exchange called money than any other single activity. It is often called "life's support system."

Money has been hailed as both an asset and a liability, as the gauge of all success and the root of all evil. Many people spend the majority of their waking hours thinking about it. To some, the lust for wealth has become so overpowering they have become virtual slaves to money, even compromising their integrity to obtain it. A successful Manhattan real estate broker is reported to have said, "I could have made much more money in my life, but I preferred to sleep well at night."

Money, or the lack of it, has been blamed for the breakup of families, the failure of businesses, and the collapse of governments. The world is still divided into the haves and have-nots.

Wealth, however, should not be viewed as a destructive force. Some of the world's greatest discoveries and creations have resulted from the simple desire of an individual to earn income. George Frederick Handel had a financial need when he secluded himself for twenty-one days and wrote *The Messiah*.

By itself, money is neither good nor bad. Currency is simply paper or metal that has been given value by a government or a financial institution. The only meaning of money is that which we personally attach to it. For example, a grandmother can place a dollar bill in the hand of a child as an expression of love. Or, money can be offered as a bribe to influence legislation.

To understand the significance of money, it is important to look at how it is treated in Scripture. One verse out of every six in Matthew, Mark, and Luke deals with finances. Many people are surprised to learn that Jesus had more to say about the proper use of money than about repentance, salvation, heaven, or any other subject.

Christ was betrayed for thirty pieces of silver. Ananias and Sapphira lied about money. Paul's ship was wrecked because of the greed of its owners.

Since we cannot escape the central role of currency in our world, how we view it is of vital importance. Here is what is clear: A beautiful estate has been established and you have been given the title of a steward. When you see yourself as "owner of nothing," your perspective dramatically changes. You're just looking after the estate. However, if you believe you have title to your possessions, you may react with overprotectiveness, fear of loss, anxiety—perhaps even anger when you feel that others don't respect what is yours.

Unfortunately, many people continue to fall into the trap of being possessed by their possessions. The way out of the trap is coming to the conclusion that God has given you all that you have. You don't own it. You've been asked to be the guardian, the caretaker.

What's Your Value?

How do we receive the money for which we are guardians? It is a direct result of providing goods or services for people. In a free enterprise system, people earn a wide range of salaries. Two children raised in the same home may earn widely divergent amounts; one may grow up to earn a minimum wage, and the other be the head of a giant corporation with a six-figure income.

While there are exceptions, most people are paid in direct proportion to their self-value. For example, if you believe in your heart of hearts that you are worth $60,000 a year, you will consciously and unconsciously work to make it so. The opposite is also true. We "self-sabotage" what we think we don't deserve. Henry Ford said, "Money doesn't change men, it merely unmasks them. If a man is naturally selfish, or arrogant, or greedy, the money brings it out; that's all."

The only people who *make* money are those who work in the minting houses of government. The rest of us *earn* money through the exchange of goods and services.

Many people, however, spend a lifetime earning an income, yet fail to follow a plan to insure financial security for the coming years. Retirement is something they wish would happen soon, but they are not prepared for it.

Take Five

Regardless of your age or income, there is something specific you can do to greatly enhance your personal economy. It is simply called "Take Five" and here's how it works. Make a decision to set aside $5 out of every $100 that comes your way. Invest it immediately, and allow the interest to be added to the principal. It may require a revision of your budget, but you'll be amazed at what will happen.

Here's an example. If an individual or a young couple earns $30,000 annually at the age of twenty-five, the investment the first year would be $1,500. At a 7 percent interest rate, they would earn an additional $105 on that sum the first year. Even if they *never* received a raise or a promotion and still made the same $30,000 a year when they retired, at age sixty-five their little plan would produce a nest egg of $340,000. It doesn't take a math wizard to figure out that the same person, receiving normal wage increases over a lifetime and investing 5 percent and having it yield 7 percent would amass over one million dollars using the Take Five plan.

Financial success will be determined by a change in your lifestyle and also by the way in which you view money. When you realize that seeds are for planting rather than for eating, there will be a bumper crop at harvesttime. A motto on the office wall of a New York stockbroker reads, "To turn $100 into $110 is work. To turn $100 million into $110 million is inevitable."

Why don't people do it? They have not made a commitment to treat investing as they treat other areas of life. John Jacob Astor said, "Wealth is largely the result of habit." When you consistently invest in your future, an amazing process begins. The result leads to a level of financial security that translates into self-confidence and a personal optimism about tomorrow.

The road will not always be smooth, but the results will be worth it. The children of Israel knew what it was to struggle, but "He also brought them out with silver and gold, and there was none feeble among His tribes" (Ps. 105:37). They struggled, but they were rewarded.

This is the time to make a personal declaration that you will never allow a week to pass without making a financial investment in your future.

your newborn body

"Lose Twenty Pounds on the Grapefruit Diet!"
"The Amazing High Fiber Cure!"
"How Niacin Can Add Years to Your Life!"

A quick glance of the magazine covers at a supermarket checkout counter reveals much about our fixation with personal health. Enough diets are introduced each year to allow a person to try a new one every week. And it seems that some people do.

Our interest in physical fitness, however, is not new. Nearly two thousand years ago Plutarch was giving medical advice. He said, "A man ought to handle his body like the sail of a ship, and neither lower or reduce it much when no cloud is in sight, nor be slack and careless in managing it when he comes to suspect something is wrong."

Instead of following Plutarch's balanced approach to life, many people are unstable in regard to diet, exercise, and their physical health.

Interaction of Mind and Body

While every case has its unique factors, the majority of physicians agree that the mind plays a significant role in your well-being. European researcher Johan Algrist says, "To deny the possibility of close links between mental state and immunological reactions ought to be regarded as scientific suicide."

We are learning that the mind has a large impact on physical health. Every thought produces a physiological response that alters our chemical balance to some degree. Dr. Steven Locke, professor at Harvard Medical School, in his book, *The Healer Within*, agrees.

> Psychological factors can play a part in causing disease—all the way from colds to cancer. . . . Researchers now have some information about the way thoughts and moods set in motion a ballet of hormones, neurotransmitters, and nerve cell activity that has a subtle, but telling effect on health.[1]

The mind, when linked with our powerful emotional response system, can produce a wide range of behavior. In many cases, our actions are merely signals that denote other basic needs. Food, for example, is often used as a substitute for love, affection, and security. Case studies indicate that some individuals become overweight as an unconscious protection against intimate relationships. Many women who have been sexually abused as children are overweight.

Other people become anorexic because they always think of themselves as fat, whatever their weight.

Why Are You Dieting?

The story is told about two men in Kansas who were talking about diets when one of the men issued a challenge. He said, "I can show you a way to lose those thirty pounds faster than you ever imagined."

"Just tell me and I'll do it," said his friend.

"This plan has no diet, no pills, no exercise," he said. 'We'll start tomorrow morning."

The next day, when the overweight man arrived, his friend was waiting for him with two fifteen-pound suitcases and two pairs of handcuffs. He attached the cases to the man's wrists and said, "Wear these for two weeks and never take them off, even while you sleep, eat, or take a shower."

It took only a few hours for the man to determine how different his life would be without those thirty pounds. His friend removed the handcuffs, and the man began losing his *own* thirty pounds.

What about you? If you are one of the millions on a diet, it is important that you look closely at the reasons you want to take inches off your waistline. If, for example, you are losing weight to be accepted by others, then you are assuming that a thin body is a source of acceptance. What is the result? Another unhealthy dependency in the search for approval. Spinach, salmon, and strawberries are important because they contribute to good nutrition and physical strength, but not as a source of emotional security.

Ask three people and you'll get four suggestions for a good diet. One of the best plans of action was given years ago by a medical doctor. He said, "Eat breakfast like a king, eat lunch like a prince, but eat dinner like a pauper." He was communicating a basic principle of health. Give your body the chance to actively burn off the calories it takes in. The less food the body is required to process at night, the healthier and more rested the person becomes, and the fewer pounds are added.

If fad diets actually worked, why would it be necessary to continually invent new ones? Why are they usually a failure? Diets don't succeed because they cause people to concentrate on the very condition they want to resolve—excess food and excess weight. Since we tend to respond to our most dominating thought, being on a diet often results in eating *more* food, not less.

A New Focus

To end the yo-yo syndrome of alternating weight loss and gain, stop concentrating on food and begin to concentrate on *you*. When you begin to do things, as suggested in this book, you will enhance your perceived personal value and growth. The result will be an increased desire to look sharper and feel healthier.

Since your self-concept is rooted in your needs, it is important that you—and not your emotions—are in control of your needs. When food or anything external is in charge, you are headed in the wrong direction. Remember: The better you feel about yourself, the more you will be in control of your needs, and your body will benefit.

Often, we focus entirely on the external causes for poor health. Cancer, for example, has been blamed on everything from ice cream to microwave ovens. By focusing on these, we tend to pay far more attention to what to *avoid* than to making and living a positive plan for a quality life.

A small child asked the Sunday school teacher, "Why did people in the Bible live so much longer than we do?"

The teacher answered, "They lived longer because they didn't know they weren't supposed to." Our bodies respond to the way we're thinking, whether positive or negative.

People who make a career of physical fitness and good health know that we all need a well-balanced diet, good nutrition, and the proper amount of physical exercise for our age and circumstances. What do we accomplish by taking in the proper number of calories, if we fail to burn them away? What do we gain by eating the right amounts of food, if we don't meet nutritional requirements? When we couple nutrition with the biblical concept of emotional health, the combination produces great results. The Book of Proverbs in the Bible sums it up nicely: "Joy does good like a medicine" (Prov. 17:22).

The Secret Ingredient

Good health, of course, is not solely the result of a good diet. For a lot of people the missing element is exercise. One person is reputed to have said that the only physical activity some people get is jumping to conclusions, running down their friends, sidestepping responsibility, dodging issues, passing the buck, and pushing their luck.

Watching what you eat will not automatically produce a healthy body. A change of lifestyle that includes a daily exercise program is essential.

As a vital part of your twenty-four hour turn-around, can you make this commitment? *Starting today, I will spend a minimum of fifteen minutes every day in a regular program of physical exercise.*

You say, "That really sounds simple! Just fifteen minutes a day?" Making the resolution is easy but following it religiously is more difficult. We are, however, talking about the missing ingredient in a personal plan for your continued good health and longevity.

If your objective is nothing more than a brisk walk around the block or through a shopping mall, start now and vow to make it a daily habit. You may be surprised to find that the fifteen minutes of activity turns into a half-hour workout. Who knows? You may even buy some physical fitness equipment or join a health club.

But even if you stick with only fifteen minutes a day, it will do you good.

Remember, making exercise an obsession is not your goal. What is vital is that starting today, daily physical activity becomes a permanent part of your life. It's the secret to increased energy, a lowered risk of disease, and an overall newborn you.

the look of a winner

A businessman from Tulsa was waiting for a plane at the San Francisco airport. Suddenly, he gathered the courage to try something he had wanted to do for a long time. Taking a deep breath, he walked up to a well-dressed gentleman and said, "Sir, I wonder if you'd do me a favor."

"I'll do my best," said the stranger.

"Well, since you've never seen me before and will probably never see me again, I have a request I'd like you to help me with."

"Sure! Go ahead and ask," the man responded.

"I know this is going to sound strange, but I'd like for you to look me over and give me your honest opinion of my appearance."

The man laughed and said, "You are really serious, aren't you?"

"Yes," smiled the businessman. "Go ahead and tell me what you think. If you were me, what changes would you make?"

The stranger looked at the man and said, "Well, since you asked for it, here are my observations. There are a couple of things you might want to try. First, your glasses are a little out of style. They're not wearing rims that thick these days. Then, I'd trim off those sideburns."

"That's what I needed to hear," said the businessman, as he thanked the gentleman and boarded the plane.

The next day back in Tulsa, he paid a visit to his barber and to an eyewear shop.

Often, we are the last to discover how we really appear. We may not have the boldness to solicit the advice of a stranger, but perhaps we need to look in the mirror and ask, "What does my image communicate about me?"

John T. Molloy, in his fascinating book *Dress for Success*, conducted many research studies to learn how people respond to others based on their clothing.

In one test, Molloy wanted to know if it were true that the color of the raincoat a man wore determined how people would treat him. He showed 1,362 people, a cross section of the general public, two nearly identical photos of the same man. There was only one variable. The pictures showed the same man in the same pose, dressed in the same suit, the same shirt, the same tie, and the same shoes. The only difference was the raincoat. In one it was black and in the other light beige. Participants were told that the pictures were of twin brothers and were asked to identify the more prestigious of the two.

The results were amazing. Said Molloy, "Over 87 percent, or 1,118 people, chose the man in the beige raincoat."[1]

The general public, for some reason, identifies a black raincoat with middle- to lower-class people. They identify the upper class with beige raincoats.

Do people make instant judgments of you by what you wear? Absolutely. You do it too. A person wearing work boots, for example, is rarely visualized as a candidate for corporate management.

A Daily Checklist

It has been proven again and again that men and women who begin to dress in the style of the jobs they desire are soon viewed as potential candidates for those positions. The theory is that when people can "see" it, they can "be" it.

The question may be asked, "Was the promotion the result of the change of appearance or the result of strong goal setting and a positive self-image?" In point of fact, few people change their appearance without enhancing their self-esteem or setting new goals for themselves.

In this hour you are being asked to change your appearance, but not for the reasons you might imagine. Your goal is not to impress others but to affect you! When you prepare for the day, spend a few extra moments going through a small checklist on your looks. Ask yourself:

Is my hair arranged the best it can be?

Is my choice of clothing appropriate for today?

Are the colors and styles suitable for my activity?

Why are these small details important? When you feel proud and confident of the way you look, it translates into positive action in every situation you encounter.

A simple act such as shining your shoes can have a subtle but profound influence on your behavior. Suddenly, you feel better about yourself. You walk and speak with more authority and confidence.

Women can achieve the same effect by wearing a particular piece of jewelry. Men can wear a stylish tie.

A dab of expensive perfume or cologne may not be noticed by anyone you meet, but *you* know it is there, and it gives you an extra boost of self-esteem. Psychiatrists report a significant increase in personal value in clients who desire to be more influential and respected. In many cases, the single most effective element of progress is a change in dress to correspond with the desired image.

Most people develop a habit of dressing in a certain style and never make a substantial change in their appearance. You certainly need to be your own person, but periodically you need to make an assessment of how you compare to the world around you. A quick way to do this is to pick up a current copy of *Time* or *Newsweek*. Look at the advertisements. What are the people wearing? How are the hairstyles changing? You may not choose to mimic the ads, but an awareness of current trends gives you more choices.

What's the Cost?

When it comes to style, many people say, "I just can't afford it." Style, however, has much more to do with personal taste, cleanliness, and good grooming than with money. A millionaire with no sense of fashion or appearance is certainly not a reflection of his socioeconomic status.

The opposite may also be true. In many cases, an individual with a small clothing budget can buy a simple wardrobe at a discount store that can pass for pure elegance. It's a matter of making thoughtful choices. Plato said it long ago, "Beauty of style and harmony and grace and good rhythm depends on simplicity."

We know of a restaurant owner in Baltimore who decided to add a little class to his establishment. Instead of spending a small fortune for an interior decorator, he devised a simple plan. He painted the walls white, sprayed the ceiling and all of the chairs black, and placed a white tablecloth over each of his none-too-chic tables. He then provided each server with a white shirt, black bow tie, and black jacket. Almost instantly and without a menu change, the restaurant began to draw a more upscale clientele, and the business was a success. The black-and-white decor and the well-dressed servers presented an elegant image.

Regardless of the amount you spend on your wardrobe, the money is wasted unless you keep the garments presentable. When famed lawyer Clarence Darrow was teased about his appearance, he said, "I go to a better tailor than any of you and pay more for my clothes. The only difference is that you probably don't sleep in yours." Confidence in your appearance is a good beginning, but there is more you can do to convey a sense of poise and assurance.

Anne Colvin Winters, executive director of the National League of Junior Cotillions, a social-training program for young people, believes that self-confidence is a learned behavior. She says, "I consistently emphasize the importance of 'walking strong.'" The act of squaring your shoulders and walking with purpose should become a habit. There's no better way to look good in your stylish wardrobe.

Other Image-Changers

Have you ever had to shake hands with someone who extends his or her hand like a cold, dead fish? Recently, a man who was nearly sixty years of age confessed that for years no one had told him his handshake was like a limp rag. "It never dawned on me," he confessed, "until one day, a friend took me aside and gave me a word of friendly advice on the topic. Just think," he said, "I spent most of my adult life with a handshake that communicated weakness because I was totally unaware of my behavior. Now when I shake hands with someone I make sure my handshake is strong. I feel better about myself!"

The manner in which you speak is important too. The next time you are in a group discussion, notice who is the dominant person. It is usually the speaker who uses a low voice and speaks deliberately, enunciating clearly. The aggressive person with a loud, high voice is rarely respected as an authority.

Recently, a news anchor at a major television station in Florida was asked about his preparation as a newsman. He said, "When I was growing up, I had a horrible regional accent and mumbled most of my words." During high school, he decided that if he wanted to be a success he needed to speak like those who *were* successful. On a small battery-operated cassette, he taped the "CBS Evening News with Walter Cronkite." He said, "Every afternoon, I walked to a vacant lot near our home and practiced. I'd play a sentence and say it out loud again and again until it sounded just like Cronkite."

What was the result? He said, "My accent changed. I no longer mumbled, and before long I got a job at a local radio station reading the news."

Some people delight in speaking with a noticeable rural or ethnic accent. Yet, in most cases, their progress will be seriously hindered without a program of conscious change.

When you begin to pay special attention to the image you portray, it opens the door to new possibilities. Attending a communications workshop or joining the local chapter of Toastmasters International can help you gain confidence and portray the image you desire.

Should you imitate the dress and actions of a person you emulate? That won't be necessary *if your appearance is one that gives you a sense of personal worth*. Trying to impress others will be a waste of time and energy unless you have first become someone *you* value.

Make it a daily habit to give yourself a once-over to determine if what you see in the mirror is the best you can be. Do at least one specific thing each week to improve your image.

When you become both your toughest and best critic, you won't need to worry about what others say. This will build confidence in who you are and what you reflect. Not only will you think and feel like a winner, but *you will have the look of a winner.*

the discovery of excellence

A man with some spare cash thought he had found a bargain when he bought for $18,000 a run-down house on the south side of Chicago. He painted it inside and out, fixed the plumbing, added some landscaping, and put it on the market. To his surprise there were no offers. Finally, he asked some Realtors for advice. "What's wrong with this house?"

"It's not the house," they told him. "It's the neighborhood."

Immediately, he went to his bank and borrowed the down payment for four additional fixer-uppers on the same block. By the time the last one was painted and the final shrub was in place, something began to happen on that street. Up and down the block people brought out their paintbrushes and garden tools. In a matter of three months, home values in the neighborhood climbed dramatically.

What happened? One man made a firm commitment to go first-class and the effect was contagious.

Ten Keys to Personal Excellence

In history, the word *excellence* has been used as a title of honor. It derives from the verb *excel* which means "to go beyond average."

Many people equate quality with something costly or extravagant, but that is not always the case. What determined the difference between an antique car in mint condition and a rusted piece of junk? The answer is usually that the owner of the valuable auto spent ten dollars a year on a can of wax and took the time to keep the car clean.

When you walk into a lumberyard you see three grades of boards: Grade C, rough on both sides, full of knotholes; grade B, a little better, smooth on one side; and grade A, first quality, smooth. If the board is to be hidden by plywood or plaster, you might choose grades B or C, but if you were crafting a piece of furniture, there would be only one choice. You'd go for the quality and choose grade A.

How can the door to personal excellence be opened? Here are ten important keys.

Key One: Don't Settle for Average

Whatever your task, make it your constant goal to perform it better than you've ever done it before. Then repeat the performance again and again, until you reach the excellence that reflects your best.

Unfortunately, many have adopted a personal policy of doing just enough to get by. They think the highest goal is graduation rather than excellence. It has come as a shock to many employers that there is a wide gap between a person with a degree and one who can perform at a high level of distinction.

Mediocrity could be called the cancer of the soul. Those who practice it soon find their personality has become a mirror image of it—dull and boring.

Key Two: Pay Attention to Detail

A superior craftsman is one who encourages a close examination of his final product. He might even hand you a magnifying glass and say, "Here, take a look."

Concern for the little things is what separates the master from the novice. Pianist Arthur Schnabel said, "The notes I handle no better than many pianists. But the pauses between the notes—ah, that is where the art resides."

Whether you are an artist, a computer programmer, a dentist, or a telephone operator, never become complacent in the performance of your work. Job satisfaction is much more than the amount you earn or the promotions you receive. It comes by finding joy in the details of your work.

Key Three: Develop a Deep Commitment

People who demonstrate superior quality are those who have seen the big picture. They have a strong sense of purpose and view their task in terms of its contribution to the world.

You may wonder, "Can people who spend a lifetime making gears and axles at the Ford Motor Company be committed to their work?" Visit the plant and you'll be surprised. They are motivated by consumer safety, foreign competition, reports from the quality-control lab, and their personal productivity. For many, the longer they stay at the same job, the deeper the dedication grows.

On a scale of one to ten, give your commitment a performance rating. Make it your objective to achieve the target called "Superior."

Key Four: Be Known for Ethics and Integrity

A large retail firm in St. Louis was recently forced to lay off nearly 20 percent of its workforce. The personnel manager was asked, "How did you make the cuts? What criteria did you use?"

He said, "We looked closely at attendance, productivity, personality and the measurable signs of success or failure, but our real goal was to retain workers who were of the highest moral character. We can never replace honesty and integrity."

You can develop a reputation for enthusiasm and job skills, but it is how you pass the "ethics" exam that truly counts.

Key Five: Show Genuine Respect for Others

A restroom at a Kentucky gas station was amazingly clean. The sign above the mirror said, "Please pretend this is your own bathroom and your mother is coming for a visit! Thanks."

Excellence becomes a lifestyle only when we practice the Golden Rule without giving it a second thought. That's possible when we elevate the worth of others to the same level we hold for ourselves.

Les Giblin, an authority on human relations, says that our actions must be genuine. "You can't make the other fellow feel important in your presence if you secretly feel that he is a nobody."[1]

Key Six: Go the Second Mile

For a professional athlete, the demonstration of excellence comes much later than the dedication to become a world champion. It is a long journey from being a rookie in spring training to being inducted into the Baseball Hall of Fame, and it will only happen to the player who commits more time and effort than others are willing to give.

Our response to adversity determines our success. How do we overcome a major setback? How do we discover light in the midst of darkness? It's not the simple task but the difficult one that makes us. Excellence begins when we go beyond the call of duty, when we go the second mile. That is why we must develop resilience and learn to bounce back from failure.

Key Seven: Be Consistent

Companies that receive annual contracts from major corporations are those that produce a predictable product. They are judged by their quality, their consistency, and their conformity with previous practice.

The ability to perform again and again at a high standard doesn't come easily. It is the result of constant practice. Those who are the best never stop practicing.

Following a brilliant recital, a lady told the concert violinist, "I'd give half of my life to be able to play the violin that well."

The peformer's response—"Madam, that's exactly what I gave."

Key Eight: Never Stop Improving

Excellence is not synonymous with perfection. It does mean, however, that you are doing it right *most* of the time. You've mastered something to the point of quality. But there is always room for improvement.

Standards of excellence are not chiseled in stone. They are constantly being redefined. It is important to recognize that what was graded excellent last year may not be so this year. That is why we must keep mastering new skills.

Will Rogers said, "Let advertisers spend the same amount of money improving their product that they do on advertising, and they wouldn't have to advertise it."

The old axiom, "Practice makes perfect," is not true. Practice makes *improvement*, but the process never ends. Rehearsing adds to experience because it's an opportunity to make mistakes and learn how to do better.

Key Nine: Make Excellence a Lifestyle

Quality is not simply a word found in a certificate of achievement on your wall. It is the result of something that is alive, a part of your heart and soul. Tom Peters said in his book *A Passion for Excellence*, "Top-flight performance is not dry and deadly; it is spirited and emotion-filled."[2]

If you were asked to name five people who are known for their quality and exceptional work, who would they be? More often than not, they would be people who have made excellence a lifestyle.

Key Ten: Always Give 110 Percent

Former Secretary of State Henry Kissinger asked an assistant to prepare an analysis. The assistant worked day and night. An hour after he gave it to Kissinger, he got it back. There was a note attached that told him to redo it.

The assistant stayed up all night revising the report. Again Kissinger asked him to redo it. After rewriting the report three times, the assistant asked to see Kissinger. He told him, "I've done the best I can do."

Kissinger said, "In that case, I'll read it now."

Every task undertaken becomes a living portrait of the person who does it. It is not *what* you do, but *how well* you do it that determines the value of the portrait.

Anything worth doing is worth giving the best you have and all you can add to the task. It's worth 110 percent.

The ten keys to excellence are powerless unless they are activated. The action isn't automatic. It begins with each of us. We must turn the handle and open the door.

Pause for a moment and scan each of the keys you have just read. Which ones are the weakest, most fragile links in your chain? Decide to concentrate on strengthening them until they become solid and strong.

Excellence is a lifetime commitment worth making.

a brand-new heart

According to the National Institute of Mental Health, at least three million Americans suffer from panic disorder at some time in their lives. These people will regularly experience dramatic symptoms, among them pounding heartbeat, chest pains, terror, and fear of losing control.

Panic disorder is a real and treatable illness. You will probably never deal with such an attack. But to a greater or lesser degree, we all must deal with issues of the heart, of one sort or another.

In this hour, we are going to ask you to place the searchlight deep inside to determine what truly makes you tick.

The heart is much more than a vital part of your body that throbs with the beat of life itself. Depending on who is giving the description, the word *heart* has dozens of meanings. To an athlete it is the source of courage. To someone in love it is the source of emotion. To a spiritual person it is home to both good and evil.

A True Heart

At an early age we are taught the value of having a heart that is pure and clean. A life built on a foundation of truth has an unlimited potential, but without this foundation, there is chaos. William F. James, a founder of Boys' Town orphanage, said, "There are only three things necessary to success: first, normal intelligence; second, determination; and third, absolute honesty."

At every turn on the precarious road of life, there are difficult choices and temptations. Some people will always take the easy way out. In the words of an old adage, "The path of least resistance makes crooked rivers and crooked men."

Those who fail to tell the truth eventually pay a high price—sometimes sooner rather than later. Here is what happened to four boys in high school who walked into the classroom one hour late after lunch. They were out having fun and missed an important exam the teacher had scheduled.

"We're sorry, Mrs. James," one of the young men explained. "We had a flat tire."

"Don't worry about it," said the teacher. "I'll let you take a make-up test."

She then asked each of the boys to sit in a different corner of the room. "Take out a paper and pencil," said Mrs. James. "This is going to be a simple exam with only one question."

The young men were stunned when she asked them, "Which tire was flat?" It was a test the boys would never forget.

A Trusting Heart

While it is vital that you have a truthful heart, it is also important to have a heart that is trusting. Dr. Redford Williams, director of the Behavioral Medicine Research Center at Duke University Medical Center, in his book *The Trusting Heart*, says, "Those who have a trusting heart are more likely to remain healthy throughout most of their lives and to live long." He says that such a heart "believes in the basic goodness of humankind, that most people will be fair and kind in relationships with others."[1]

Men and women serving in the armed forces may have personal disagreements with their superiors, but if they are to survive they must develop trust in them. On a daily basis, their lives are in the hands of their superiors. And when the bombs start falling and the bullets start flying, they must know that their leaders will make wise decisions.

A Loving Heart

Throughout history, there have been those who have built their dreams on the feelings of their hearts and have known extraordinary achievement.

In 1925, two young medical school graduates and their father started a small sanitarium for mental patients on a farm outside Topeka, Kansas. This was a time when the "rest cure" was in vogue in psychiatry, and patients were sent to impersonal institutions to live out their lives.

This father and his sons had a different idea. They were determined to create a loving, family atmosphere among their patients and staff. The nurses were given special training on how to behave toward specific patients. About one they were told, "Let him know that you value and like him." About another they were instructed, "Be kind but firm with this woman; don't let her become worse."

The doctors were Karl and William Menninger, and the Menninger Clinic with such "revolutionary" methods has become world famous and has helped countless numbers of people. Dr. Karl Menninger said,

Love cures people—both the ones who give it and the ones who receive it. . . . It is this intangible thing *love*—love in many forms—which enters into every therapeutic relationship. It is an element which finds and heals, which comforts and restores, which works what we have to call, for now, miracles. . . . Love is the medicine for the sickness of mankind. We can live if we have love.

Love, the great emotion of the heart, is the key to success at every level. But like so many of life's great treasures, if we don't use it, we lose it. And the more we learn about love by loving, the greater becomes our capacity to love. Writer Katherine Anne Porter said, "Love must be learned again and again; there is no end to it. Hate needs no instruction, but wants only to be provoked."

Many become so desperate seeking love that they miss the experience of *feeling* loved. To them, the search for heartfelt affection becomes much like a hunt of foxes and hounds, played by an elaborate set of rules. The result is a mental exercise rather than an emotional experience.

It is important to realize that the heart is always ready to respond to those who will knock on its door. Mother Teresa, who became an angel of mercy to Calcutta's poor, said, "Love is a fruit in season at all times, and within reach of every hand."

If someone were asked to describe your ability to give and receive love and affection, what would they say? Would you be portrayed as a person who is ruled by your heart? Or would they describe your powers of logic and say you are ruled by your head?

Years ago George Washington Carver said, "How far you go in life depends on your being tender with the young, compassionate with the aged, sympathetic with the striving, and tolerant of the weak and the strong. Because some day in life you will have been all of these."

A Clean Heart

Many have never known the feeling of having their heart swept clean through love or forgiveness. It is like the couple in Colorado who were desperately trying to sell their home. They had dozens of people show interest, but no one made an offer.

"What's the problem?" they asked the real estate agent.

She told them, "Your home is beautiful on the exterior, but people are disappointed when they see the inside." It was true, the outside had a fresh coat of paint, but the interior looked like a pigsty.

Immediately they scrubbed, painted, and cleaned every room. Within three weeks they had an offer that was exactly the price they had hoped for.

So it is with our hearts. Until we become clean on the inside, our attempts to display a clean facade will have little effect. Only through spiritual transformation will our hearts become clean.

Millions of people can attest to the fact that what is described as personal faith or a conversion experience is not the result of a lifetime of searching, but rather a specific moment of transformation. Many have scoffed at the notion of instant salvation or a born-again experience, but those who have encountered such a change don't worry about the critics. They know what it means to be transformed from the inside out.

People recovering from past trauma, physical or psychological illnesses, or addictions experience a similar phenomenon. While it is certainly true that the process of cleansing and healing is sometimes slow and deliberate, it is a fact that there is a moment or an instant that many can describe as the place or the time that they knew beyond any doubt that their turn-around had taken place.

A Heart Checkup

When you become comfortable and secure with issues of the heart, your confidence spills over into every other area of activity. William Faulkner wrote: "I have found that the greatest help in meeting any problem with decency and self-respect, and whatever courage is demanded, is to know where you yourself stand."

Many of us tend to define life by the things we abhor. But when we communicate what we are *for*, in the most positive terms possible, we empower ourselves to go forward.

We all have the ability to make a fresh new start, over and over again. When we have failed, we can ask for forgiveness. And, like children learning to walk, we can rise to our feet and try once more.

You don't have to call the local hospital to schedule a heart examination. It is something you can do instantly, by yourself. What should your checkup include? Ask yourself these questions: Am I applying the Golden Rule: "Just as you want men to do to you, you also do to them likewise" (Luke 6:31)? Am I willing to forgive? Am I able to receive forgiveness? Do I care about others? According to the law of sowing and reaping, what you do for others is what you receive. Don't wait for the residue to build and build until it's time for major surgery. A change of heart will cause the rivers of life to flow freely in you. Make a pledge to yourself that you will begin each day by cleaning your heart. If it is filled with anger, determine to forgive. If it is filled with envy, look for ways to be charitable, respectful, and appreciative. If it is filled with conflict and stress, take time to relax and pray.

A sign painted on a service station in Seattle read, "A clean engine always delivers power." That's how you will be able to describe your new heart.

from master to servant

The world is overpopulated with self-serving people. Their vocabulary is filled with "I" and "me." These people will never have a servant attitude without a transition in their thinking. If you would have a change of attitude you must develop a new view of yourself and a willingness to treat others with love and forgiveness. You'll find that this transformation is not only good for those in contact with you, but it's good for you too.

A startling study makes the point clear. Social psychologist Larry Scherwitz at the Medical Research Institute of San Francisco discovered that there is a link between self-centered behavior and heart disease. Scherwitz reports, "The people who referred to themselves using pronouns *I*, *me*, and *my* most often in an interview [who were talking about themselves the most] were more likely to develop coronary heart disease, even when other health-threatening behaviors were controlled."[1]

People need to realize that ultimate achievement is not found in being called "master." The highest goals in life, health, and personal success are reached by those who choose to serve.

The Team That Wins

Dean Ornish, a medical doctor at the University of California at San Francisco, believes that servanthood plays a great role in healing. Author of *Stress, Diet, and Your Heart,* Dr. Ornish says that many heart patients see themselves as isolated, which can lead to stress and more illness. He encourages them to get involved in doing things for others. For example, he once asked two patients who disliked each other to do each other's laundry. Such selfless acts, Ornish believes, promote our ability to become well.

Learning the art of serving is easier when you see yourself as part of a team that wins because it doesn't care who gets the credit. This is true in sports and also in music. Someone asked the conductor of a great symphony orchestra which instrument he considered the most difficult to play. The conductor thought for a moment and said, "Second fiddle. I can get plenty of first violinists. But to find one who can play second fiddle with enthusiasm— that's a problem. And if we have no second fiddles, we have no harmony."

Ask any business forecaster and you'll learn that the growth industries of the future are not in manufacturing, but in service. Entrepreneur William Lear agrees. "I would say a young man has a better chance if he has an idea for a service. He won't require any machinery to execute his idea," says Lear.

Regardless of how important your enterprise becomes, if you forget to serve, you'll be like a tennis player without a racquet.

Doctors Charles and William Mayo are remembered for founding the famous Mayo Clinic in Rochester, Minnesota. Dr. Charlie, as he was called, once was host to a noble English visitor in his home. Before retiring for the night, the visitor put his shoes outside the door, expecting a servant to shine them.

The next morning the shoes were waxed, polished, and gleaming brightly. Dr. Charlie had shined them himself.

Being a servant requires a heart of love. Perhaps it was best described by St. Augustine. When he was asked, "What does love look like?" He answered, "It has the hands to help others. It has the feet to hasten to the poor and needy. It has eyes to see misery and want. It has the ears to hear the sighs and sorrows of men. That's what love looks like."

Forgiving and Forgetting

Many people can never make the transition from master to servant because they refuse to forgive. They harbor personal grudges and fail to forget past mistakes. A person who says, "I can forgive, but I cannot forget," is really saying, "I refuse to forgive."

Of that approach, author and speaker Josh McDowell says, "When I refuse to forgive, I am burning a bridge that someday I will need to pass over."

Some people never seem to learn. While visiting with a friend over coffee one morning, a young woman complained, "Every time my husband and I get into an argument, he gets historical."

The friend interrupted, "Don't you mean hysterical?"

"No, I mean historical," the lady replied. "He always brings up the past."

It's easy to laugh, but the story is tragically true. Our relationships are often hindered by past hurts that have never been made right.

What is the solution? To apologize. Norman Vincent Peale said,

A true apology is more than just acknowledgment of a mistake. It is a recognition that something you have said or done has damaged a relationship and that you care enough about the relationship to want it repaired and restored.

A successful executive in Illinois has a four-word solution to conflict. When customers or business associates present a grievance, he meets them, often in their own offices or residences, and asks, "Will you forgive me?"

Those words, coming directly from the president of the company, have a powerful effect. In nearly all of the cases, the injured party accepts the apology and the issue is dropped.

Givers and Takers

Personal change begins when we stop blaming others. People who develop a habit of blame-placing are really saying, "My life is the product of the actions of other people."

If you want to develop the heart of a servant, quickly push aside the negative events that pass your way. As an Arab proverb says, "Write the wrongs that are done to you in sand, but write the good things that happen to you on marble." We should release all feelings of resentment or inclinations to retaliation, which pull us down, and hold on to gratitude and joy, which elevate us.

A servant is a giver rather than a taker. Perhaps we should be reminded of the ancient king who requested that his corpse be displayed with his hands stretched open, holding nothing in his palms. This attitude of giving should also be ours. Since we can't take it with us, why not share it now?

Scripture tells us, "As he came from his mother's womb, naked shall he return, to go as he came; and he shall take nothing from his labor, which he may carry away in his hand" (Eccles. 5:15).

In his book *The Art of Loving*, renowned psychologist Erich Fromm summarizes what life for him is all about.

> For the productive character, giving has an entirely different meaning. Giving is the highest expression of potency. In the very act of giving, I experience my strength, my wealth, my power. This experience of heightened vitality and potency fills me with joy. I experience myself as overflowing, spending, alive, hence as joyous. Giving is more joyous than receiving, not because it is a deprivation, but because in the act of giving lies the expression of my aliveness.[2]

We must be careful to note that there is a difference between true servanthood and codependency. If you are doing for others in order to get your own needs met, then your motive comes from a personal need to be needed. Without a strong sense of personal identity, you are susceptible to becoming emotionally dependent on the approval of others. Not only does this postpone your turn-around, it enables those whom you think you are helping to become dependent on you and thus become irresponsible. That's codependency.

We are to bear one another's burdens, but there is also the time to "let each one examine his own work, and then he will have rejoicing in himself alone, and not in another" (Gal. 6:4).

A true servant often gives without the recipient knowing the donor. One day a businessman in Missouri, who regularly asked the help of a certain porter at the airport, reached his hand into his pocket to give a tip. He was dismayed to find he had no cash.

"Don't worry," said the porter as he lifted the man's suitcases. "If I can't help a friend without expecting something in return, I shouldn't even be working here."

Several months later, on Christmas Eve, the businessman found the address of the porter and drove to his home. He knocked on the door and when a child answered the man said, "Merry Christmas. Give this to your father." Then he walked away. Folded inside an unsigned Christmas card were five crisp one-hundred-dollar bills.

A verse in the Talmud says, "He who gives should never remember; he who receives should never forget."

People who give from their hearts will always be rewarded. We can heed the words of an old saying, "Takers eat well, but givers sleep well."

At times you may feel that you have nothing of significance to give, but that isn't true. When you give of yourself, you have given the greatest gift of all. It pays greater dividends than you expect. Dale Carnegie said, "You can make more friends in two months by becoming more interested in other people than you can in two years by trying to get people interested in you."[3]

If there is one sentence you should commit to memory it is this: *How can I help you?* Make it your goal to ask that question as many times each day as possible. It is the surest route to becoming a servant.

To a corporate president say, "How can I help you?"

To a neighbor on your street say, "How can I help you?" To a little child say, "How can I help you?"

Even before hearing the answer, you receive the great reward of knowing you're a giver. It's therapy that works both ways.

Every morning before going to his office, an automobile dealer in Ohio places something in his pocket that he plans to give away. It may be a ballpoint pen, a little trinket, or even a ten-dollar bill. As the day moves forward, he looks for someone he feels deserves the gift. "By constantly looking for the opportunity to give, I have a wonderful day," he said.

Those who have successfully made the transformation from being a master to being a servant know the satisfaction it brings. It should become your goal too.

Here's a checklist to measure your progress today.

Will my decisions benefit others more than myself?

Will I demonstrate that I am part of a team?

Will I avoid blaming others for my mistakes?

Will I be quick to forgive?

Will I give more than I receive?

Will my actions reflect a servant's heart?

a lifestyle of laughter

"I wish I had been born with a sense of humor," Bill told his counselor.

"Why is that important?" was the response.

"At work I am always being told that I take everything too seriously."

When Bill learned what others thought about him, he was determined to do something about it. But the first thing he needed to learn is that a sense of humor is not something we are born with, but something that we develop.

We need to recognize that humor doesn't mean telling jokes all day. Adding laughter to your life doesn't mean walking around with a grin on your face.

We need to lighten up in our approach to life. There is enough to be serious about—employment, crime, health, family relationships, finances. The list is seemingly endless. Without a coping strategy like personal humor, the burdens of life become exceedingly heavy.

According to medical science, laughter has a special role to play in good health. It causes you to inhale and exhale in short bursts, and that increases the oxygen to your lungs and bloodstream. Physicians point out that laughter causes low blood pressure to rise and high blood pressure to decrease. It even enhances blood circulation. Best of all, it lifts your spirits, relieves anxiety and, like magic, helps depression disappear.

Popular author Bernie Siegel calls laughter an "internal massage." He says, "All the muscles of the chest, abdomen and face get a little workout, and if the joke is a real knee-slapper, even the arms and legs reap the benefits."[1]

The value of a good laugh has long been recognized. Aristotle called it "a bodily exercise precious to health." A proverb from the Bible says, "A merry heart does good, like medicine, but a broken spirit dries the bones" (Prov. 17:22). And physician James Wolsh says, "People who laugh live longer than those who do not or cannot."

Perhaps *Reader's Digest* has been right all these years, calling laughter "the best medicine."

When it comes to expressing mirth with our voice, laughter distinguishes man from all other creation. And when we look around, God himself must have had a sense of humor. Can you imagine what it was like to design a giraffe? The ostrich must have drawn a few smiles too.

Today, with dozens of television programs devoted to comedy, we are surrounded by humor, but few people use it as an extension of their personality. Here are some specific ways that you can participate with those who enjoy a lifestyle of laughter.

Learn to Smile Quickly

Don't wait for someone else to smile before you respond. Lead the way. Pianist Victor Borge said, "A smile is the shortest distance between two people."

People who go through life with a perpetual frown are creating more problems than they realize. Frowns don't produce friends, but they do produce wrinkles. There is no need to look old before your time when a smile can produce amazing results. As the words on a bumper sticker state, "A smile is a good way to kill time between disasters." Let the world know that something good is happening to you. Remember the song and "put on a happy face."

Relax!

Perhaps the quickest way to relax is to be around people who have humor to share. You don't have to try to be funny; just enjoy those who are. Experts who measure such things say the relaxation response after a good laugh lasts up to forty-five minutes. Relaxed muscles cannot coexist with anxiety. Laughter is a wise choice.

At a recent seminar, participants were asked to turn to their neighbors and pay one sincere compliment. Within seconds the entire room was filled with laughter. Then the leader asked several people to stand and repeat the compliments they gave. In an environment of good humor, the audience fully relaxed.

Become a Child Again

A popular theme in current recovery books is rediscovering the "inner child"—the child we once were. Instead of repressing those childlike urges, go ahead and let them out. Training leaders for corporations know the value of "playtime" for adults as a balance for the serious material they are asked to learn.

An ad agency in Chicago schedules weekly "Show and Tell" sessions for their employees to share the projects they are working on. By pretending they are in the first grade, everybody has a great deal of fun—and learns in the process.

Jesus said, "Unless you are converted and become as little children, you will by no means enter the Kingdom of heaven" (Matt. 18:3). He knew that the child in us has unlimited faith, trust, and creativity.

We should never be embarrassed or ashamed to laugh and enjoy youthful fun. The child we once were not only still exists inside us but deserves authentic expression at appropriate times in our lives.

Surround Yourself with Happy, Positive People

No law states that we must constantly be in the company of grumps. Since we have the right to choose our friends, we can decide to spend time with people who are basically happy and optimistic.

An accountant in her thirties was referred to counseling because she was often complaining about being depressed. She said, "All my life I have had an outgoing personality, but I find it difficult to smile anymore."

It did not take long to learn that for two years she had been sharing an office with another employee who was a solemn workaholic. He rarely spoke and never smiled. The dull worker wasn't unhappy—that was just his personality. But the effect on the once-enthusiastic person was devastating.

The problem was easily solved. The accountant asked her manager to switch her office. In her new working environment, her old good humor returned.

Does it make a difference with whom you spend your time? Without question.

Use Quick Humor

Think about your funny friends. In most cases they make you laugh with their clever, spontaneous remarks rather than by telling long, involved stories.

Often, a person who is making a stab at humor will spend an hour practicing and memorizing a joke or funny story to tell to friends at lunch. That person is dismayed when his friends look bored and the punch line falls flat.

Instead, try a short, short story that flows from what you are doing. For example, when you are looking at a menu, you might say, "I heard about an American who went to Madrid and wanted to order steak and mushrooms. So he drew a picture of a cow and a mushroom. What he got was a ticket to a bullfight and an umbrella."

Your friends are likely to pick up the tone and join in with one or two stories of their own.

Avoid Off-Color Humor

People who tell jokes with sexual themes communicate more about themselves than they know. Those who tell such stories, especially in the workplace, are asking for trouble. Recent sexual harassment cases have concluded that unwanted "jokes" are an intrusion on the rights of an individual.

Humor based on racial or ethnic themes falls into the same category. The rule, "When in doubt, don't do it!" is a good one to follow.

You say, "I don't tell such stories, but how should I respond when they are told?"

If you laugh uproariously, you become a participant in the telling of the offensive tale. Instead, without response or emotion, quietly walk away or change the topic. The person telling the joke and the others listening will likely get the message.

Enjoy Your Gift of Laughter

Good humor is not something to be quietly enjoyed. We each have a unique "laugh box" that is ours and ours alone. It's like our fingerprint or our signature.

Go ahead and use it with gusto. After all, you enjoy hearing the laughter of others. Enjoy your own too! A smile has its place, but so does a spontaneous laugh. Don't keep it hidden.

Make it your priority to develop your gift of laughter. You can start by trying to bring a smile to someone's face. Once that has been accomplished, take it one step further. Share a comment that will make someone laugh out loud.

The physical and emotional benefits of laughter are too valuable to pass by. If for no other reason than your good health, determine that humor is going to be a permanent part of your day.

When you stop taking life so seriously, both you and those you meet will make the world a more pleasant place.

up with enthusiasm!

When people think of legendary football coaches, they nearly always mention Vince Lombardi. When he took over the Green Bay Packers in 1959, they were at the bottom of the standings. The previous year they lost ten out of their twelve games, tied one, and won one.

Lombardi stood before his players and said, "Gentlemen, we are going to have a football team. We are going to win some games. Get that!"

What was the game plan?

Lombardi looked at his men and said, "You are going to learn to block, run, and tackle. You are going to outplay all the teams that come up against you."

Then he threw in the clincher! With more of a command than a suggestion, he ordered, "You are to have confidence in me and enthusiasm for my system. Hereafter, I want you to think of only three things: your home, your religion, and the Green Bay Packers. Let enthusiasm take hold of you."[1]

Lombardi was a master at meshing individual stars into an awesome team. He knew it would be impossible for the Packers to win against stiff NFL competition unless each player performed like an all-pro week after week.

He drilled one message into his players before every game. They could hear the words ringing in their helmets. "If you aren't fired with enthusiasm, you will be fired with enthusiasm."

They got the message.

Bubbling with Energy

Without question, the quality that separates winners from also-rans in our society is the inner fire of enthusiasm. You never have to guess whether people have such a quality. It is obvious in everything they do.

Everyone likes excitement. When people bubble with personal energy, others enjoy being around them. Business firms like to hire a staff that brings zest to the establishment. Some national restaurant chains, for example, train their staff to form an impromptu ensemble and sing "Happy Birthday" or "Happy Anniversary" to their customers on special occasions. It produces more than noise. People keep coming back.

One restaurant, knowing how people respond to excitement, devised a special plan. When a customer ordered a steak dinner, the chef placed the meal on a hot steel plate. Then, just before the waiter left the kitchen, he would drop an ice cube on the platter.

The waiter was instructed, "Walk slowly to the table. We want everyone to hear the sound of that hot platter." It wasn't the steak that was sizzling, but the ice. The plan worked like instant advertising. If customers were in the process of ordering, they'd hear that sound and choose a steak. The sizzle produced the sale.

Henry Ford built a giant automotive empire, and he knew what it took to produce results. "Enthusiasm is at the bottom of all progress! With it, there is accomplishment," said Ford. "Without it, there are only alibis."

Today, large corporations spend millions in an attempt to inspire their employees. To spark sales, they offer incentives from resort vacations to expensive jewelry. Many companies have learned, however, that a small group of people usually wins most of the prizes again and again. They are the team members who apply enthusiasm and excitement to whatever they do. They are like Mark Twain, who was once asked the reason for his success. He replied, "I was born excited."

Like an Eagle

We all came kicking and screaming into the world. But it didn't take long for people to calm us down and sing us to sleep.

Later, when we showed signs of wanting to fly like an eagle, we were told that it would be better to color within the lines, stay out of mud puddles, marry a hometown person, settle down near Mom and Dad, and get a job at the local factory. The fire of our enthusiasm was doused with a wet blanket over and over again.

It's not too late to rekindle the flame. There are still new worlds to conquer and new causes to champion. Nothing can take the place of a creative concept teamed with a person of vision and passion. Tom Watson, founder of IBM, said, "The great accomplishments of man have resulted from the transmission of ideas and enthusiasm."

Zig Ziglar set sales records for a national company before becoming an author and premier motivational speaker. He reached his goals through personal excitement that came to the surface with every presentation. In his book, *Secrets of Closing the Sale*, Ziglar says, "For every sale you miss because you're too enthusiastic, you will miss a hundred because you're not enthusiastic enough."

When Charlotte Ford, wealthy daughter of Henry Ford, was asked why she became excited about creating her own highly regarded line of women's fashions, she said, "Because getting up in the morning and having something to do is terrific."

Can a person with a self-produced enthusiasm using the "fake it till you make it" approach be as effective as a person with natural energy? There is no right or wrong when it comes to presenting yourself with gusto and zest. It's a desired trait, no matter how you produce it.

Here is what we *do* know about enthusiastic people. Anybody who can become excited about an idea, for *any* reason, can become excited about it repeatedly. Like any other learned behavior, enthusiasm can be self-created over and over again until the style of life becomes habit-forming and a permanent part of a personality.

Many excellent public speakers weren't born that way. In some cases, they used to be frightened to speak before an audience and had to tackle the problem head-on. By forcing themselves to become excited and dynamic in front of a group, they learned that they could conquer the stage. What was their greatest fear became the arena of their greatest freedom.

Maintaining Enthusiasm

Once you have proven to yourself that you can add excitement to your activity, don't allow people to stifle your zeal. An advertising executive, tired of seeing people throw wet blankets on each other, compiled a list of fail-safe phrases guaranteed to put the brakes on enthusiasm. When someone is feeling fired up, just one of these statements can dampen his spirits. The list includes:

"Might be better if . . ."

"I like it—it's just that . . ."

"I see your point, but . . ."

"Let's look at it this way."

"Our usual procedure is . . ."

"How would we justify it?"

"Yes, but . . ."

"Let me sleep on it."

You've probably met people who have used those phrases on you. The next time it happens, recognize what is taking place, and don't allow it to slow your excitement.

When you choose to add enthusiasm to your life, people immediately recognize it and often comment on it. They'll say, "She's full of life," or "He adds excitement to everything he does."

You would have to conduct a considerable search to find an individual who is both enthusiastic and pessimistic. That combination just doesn't work. When you're enthusiastic, your attitude is affected. Says author Denis Waitley, "Enthusiasm is contagious. It's difficult to remain neutral or indifferent in the presence of a positive thinker."

What is the primary cause of personal excitement? Historian Arnold Toynbee wrote, "Enthusiasm can be aroused by two things: first, an idea which takes the imagination by storm; and second, a definite, intelligible plan for carrying that idea into action."

There are, however, times when you need to recharge your batteries. How do you do this? Nothing is automatic. To keep the fire burning, you need to feed it with new activities, new dreams, and new goals.

There is a better approach to becoming animated and enthusiastic than waking up each morning and giving yourself a pep talk.

Lectures and generalities don't tend to work very well. Instead, choose one specific item on your schedule that needs a special passion or zeal to be successfully accomplished. Today concentrate on that one particular issue. Repeat the process each new day.

When you prove that you can get stirred up about one topic, you can become enthused about something else. Your goal should be to make enthusiasm a total and permanent part of everything you do.

22

your key to daily renewal

"I despise my job," a new salesclerk told her friend.

"What seems to be the problem?" the friend responded.

"The company treats me like a child," he said. "They tell me exactly what I am supposed to wear, what I am supposed to say, when I can have lunch, even when I can go to the bathroom." She added, "When I think about it, I don't even want to get up in the morning!"

This salesclerk is not alone. Countless people are employed at tasks they didn't choose, working for people they don't basically like, and often dealing with customers they wouldn't want as friends.

Those who punch a clock in factories, in retail sales, in restaurants, and dozens of other occupations face the problem of daily motivation. For others, the problem of daily motivation is more serious. What about a woman who quits her job to start a local antique store—or the man who strikes out on his own with a small used-car lot? Those who choose to become self-employed entrepreneurs have an even greater dilemma. What will happen if they call in sick? How will they pay their bills if they sleep until noon? Their daily motivation may determine the success or failure of their businesses.

Regardless of their occupations and daily chores, people echo the same questions. "How can I cope?" "Where can I find the strength to face another day?"

Your Mission Statement

The key to daily renewal is the same for an individual as for a large organization. Both must ask and answer this question: *What is my mission statement?*

Have you ever taken the time to put into words the purpose and work of your life? When you do that, you will begin to realize how your daily responsibilities fit into your larger plan.

Your personal mission statement might include statements such as:

1. I will place family before business.
2. I will never compromise my ethics.
3. I will develop a new proficiency this year.
4. I will concentrate on my immediate tasks.
5. I will always seek God's will before making decisions.

Positive things will happen when you are clearly focused. Author Elbert Hubbard told the story of an incident during the Spanish-American War. It was imperative that the president get a message to the leader of the insurgents. His name was Garcia and he was known to be somewhere in the mountains of Cuba, one of the battlegrounds of the war. But no mail or telegraph could reach him.

Someone said, "There's a fellow by the name of Rowan who will find Garcia for you, if anybody can."

Rowan took the letter without hesitation. He sealed it in a leather pouch strapped over his heart. He landed in the dark of night off the coast of Cuba and made his way to the mountains and, after much difficulty, found Garcia. He handed him the letter, turned around, and headed home.

Hubbard tells this story in "A Message to Garcia." It's an inspiration to those who value hard work. Rowan didn't ask, "Exactly where is he?" He didn't say, "I doubt if I can do it." He refused to complain. There was a job to be done and he did it.[1]

Instead of making a dozen excuses why you can't do the job, think about Rowan. Whatever your task, make the commitment that you are going to complete it.

When you have a clear idea of where you are headed, you worry less and less about daily distractions. You stop blaming the weather, your friends, the economy, or other forces for the situations in which you find yourself. You can even begin to repeat the words of Napoleon Bonaparte, "Circumstances! What are circumstances? I *make* circumstances!"

Take Ownership

Those who only look to external sources for their help will be disappointed. Reading the words of an inspirational writer has great value, and being challenged by a spiritual leader or motivational speaker is beneficial, but it is only when a concept, a cause, or a vision becomes *yours* that a fundamental change happens in your life. When you take ownership of a dream, it becomes a driving force that will cause you to bounce out of bed each day.

On the other hand, there are those who believe that the obstacles they face are like mines in a battlefield. They have drawn the wrong conclusion. The problems they encounter are not always enemies who stalk them waiting to attack. Instead, the problems are all too often residing on the inside, in their attitudes and expectations.

There is no anxiety or depression "out there." Neither hides in the darkness waiting to strike. Some people speak as if fear resides in every airplane, and the moment they get on board it will suddenly reach out and envelop them. That's not how it works. Fear is not lurking on the jumbo jet. It is a matter of your own perception.

What about beauty or joy or success? They too are not found in the outside world but are "in the eye of the beholder." They are in the heart and soul. As Eric Hoffer said, "When people are bored, it is primarily with their own selves they are bored."

How you think about your task has everything to do with how you approach it. The salesclerk who sees her job as regimented, almost forced labor, lives in a state of perpetual gloom. The moment she begins to see how her work plays an important part in providing for her physical needs, developing her skills, and serving people, her outlook can drastically change.

Wayne Dyer, author of *The Sky's the Limit*, says, "Thoughts are everything." Before they become reality, however, a three-step process is involved.

First we encounter knowledge. Next the knowledge stimulates thoughts. Finally, our thoughts become things.

How real are our thoughts? Those who study the patterns of our mind tell us that what is, simply *is*. But when we give it attention, it multiplies and grows. In the same way, what we resist persists. When we try to eradicate a problem by cutting it out of our lives, we'd do well to remember what happens when we prune a tree. The fruit or flower just becomes larger. Most important is that you take ownership and personal control of your thought-life.

Prayer and Meditation

Self-renewal can be greatly enhanced by deep inner reflections. That is why it is important to set aside some time each day to be alone to focus on your thoughts.

The mind is capable of receiving an overwhelming amount of stimuli. Sometimes it is necessary to focus the mind in order to selectively direct this mental ability toward a certain goal with singleness of purpose. In our complex and hurried society, prayer and meditation have proven to be effective as a means of focus and concentration. Talking to God in prayer about our concerns and listening for his answers through meditation are important steps in personal renewal.

Before Christ inaugurated his ministry, he spent forty days alone in the desert (Matt. 4:1–11). Just prior to choosing the twelve disciples, he spent the entire night alone in the hills (Luke 6:12). The night before the cross, he sought the quiet of the Garden of Gethsemane (Matt. 26:36–46).

Richard Foster, author of *Celebration of Discipline*, calls meditation "a classic Christian discipline." The psalmist said, "Blessed is the man . . . [whose] delight is in the law of the LORD, and in His law he meditates day and night" (Ps. 1:1–2).

Beyond entering into contemplation to empty your mind or to detach yourself from the world, your objective should be something more. Renewal involves depending on God and being inspired by his creativity. It's much better to fill your thoughts with ideas that will move your mission forward—ideas that attach you to exciting potentials.

Solitude is important, but it must be followed by action before we see its tangible benefits. Being renewed without giving it expression is like memorizing someone's birthday, yet never sending a card. A tiny bird can watch its mother soar and fly, and even think about flying; but only when the fledgling ventures out of the nest and spreads its wings will it experience flight.

Those who realize the importance of daily renewal concentrate on what works best for them. A woman who sells commercial real estate in Philadelphia said, "Every morning, before going to work, I spend a moment recreating a large deal I have closed. Then I go out and try to make it happen again."

A successful writer once confessed that the most terrifying thing for him was a blank piece of paper in the typewriter. So he developed a plan to help solve the problem. Each day, when he was ready to stop writing, he would leave a piece of paper in the typewriter with a sentence half finished on it. The next morning, the first thing he would do was to finish that sentence. Soon he would be thoroughly engrossed in his writing and ready for a productive day.

Others deliberately attempt to shake up their creative juices by doing old things in new ways. As William Danforth said, "The best cure for a sluggish mind is to disturb its routine."

Starting Over

A successful salesman had another approach to getting motivated. When asked why he was able to achieve such positive results, he said, "I tell myself every night when I go to bed that I lost my job and tomorrow I must start from scratch." He explained that he did this because "a person in a new job always gives his best."

Henry David Thoreau used to lie in bed for a while in the morning telling himself all the good news he could think of—that he had a healthy body, his mind was alert, his work was interesting, the future looked bright, and a lot of people trusted him. Then he would rise to face the day in a world filled for him with good things, wonderful people, and exciting opportunities. By activating enthusiasm before starting his day, Thoreau set his own agenda for success.

Daily renewal is not automatic; it requires thought and action. When you have developed the big picture for the mission of your life, you are ready to do something each day to see it fulfilled. A simple method is to begin with a positive affirmation, a "Today I will . . ." thought.

You can think or even speak aloud your intention. "Today I will make a new friend." Or, "Today I will find a problem to smile at—and resolve."

As you move through your routine, constantly remind yourself to follow through on your objective. Follow-through works in golf, in tennis, and in life. Then, before you fall asleep each night, you'll be able to say, "I did my best."

The Creator gave us springtime to let us know we can be renewed. That is when flowers and plants burst out all around us. Animals shed their winter coats, come out from hibernation, and give birth to new offspring.

For you and me, however, springtime is not designed to be an annual affair but a daily discipline.

the power of persistence

For years, people have responded to magazines offering "The Lazy Man's Way to Riches," or "You Can Earn a Fortune in Your Spare Time." Most people know these empty promises are a contradiction in terms. You can't get something for nothing. But they sure hope they can.

If the growth of the lottery industry in America is any indication, most people would like to become wealthy without the hassle of physical labor. Some workers do just enough on the job to avoid being terminated, and they are paid just enough to keep them from leaving.

A young carryout boy at a food store in Seattle was asked, "How long have you been working here?"

He laughed and replied, "Ever since they threatened to fire me!"

Those who wonder why so few people become successful don't have to look far for the answer. You need only to stand at the door of a large manufacturing plant at the end of a shift to find out.

When the whistle blows, hundreds of people bolt for the exits like cattle coming out of a chute. If you don't move quickly, you'll be crushed in the stampede.

There are some select people, however, who approach work with an entirely different strategy. They know exactly where they are headed, and every day brings them closer to their goals. If they plan to grow with their present firm, they stay behind a few extra minutes to discuss the work with their superiors. If they are planning to move to another company, they demonstrate their dedication so they will have a solid, favorable recommendation. Others, who want to start their own businesses, work extra hours whenever possible to set some funds aside.

Whatever your objective, there's one sure way to accomplish it. Make certain that you do something every day that brings you closer to its realization.

It's Worth the Time It Takes

When you examine the record of those who are lauded as having achieved great success, you see that their empires have usually been built in one of three ways:

1. They inherited the funds from their family.
2. They were fortunate to be in the right place at the right time.
3. They had an idea and worked at it diligently until the plan succeeded.

Luck and inheritance are unreliable and outside of our control. Therefore, the third category holds the greatest promise of success. The people in this category demonstrated the power of persistence.

Sam Walton did not become an overnight giant of the retail industry. He opened a small discount store, Wal-Mart, in Bentonville,

Arkansas, and demonstrated that low prices and friendly, motivated employees would attract customers. With a carefully calculated plan, he slowly began to build new stores in an ever-widening circle until his company became the largest and most profitable discount retailer in the nation.

Corporations such as Wal-Mart, which are built in part on the principle of "growth from within," are filled with successful people who have risen from sweeping the floors to becoming vice presidents. They did quality work that was recognized by their superiors, and they were promoted. Indira Gandhi said, "My grandfather once told me that there were two kinds of people: those who do the work and those who take the credit. He told me to try to be in the first group; there was much less competition."

Whether you decide to make a career out of an occupation with a corporation, or have dreams of starting your own enterprise, be prepared to do whatever it takes—for as long as it takes—until your goal is achieved. Sometimes it takes longer than expected. Webster worked thirty-six years to produce the first edition of the dictionary that bears his name. Gibbon spent twenty-six years writing *The Decline and Fall of the Roman Empire*.

What should you do when you have tried your best, but things don't seem to be materializing? Keep hammering away. Jacob Riis, a newsman and social reformer, spent decades fighting poverty in New York City. He shared his vision with anyone who would listen but sometimes would become discouraged by the results. During those moments of despair, Riis said:

> When nothing seems to help, I go and look at a stonecutter hammering away at his huge rock. He hits it perhaps one hundred times without as much as a crack showing in it. Yet the one-hundred-and-first time will split it in two. I know that it was not that blow that did it, but all that had gone before.

In 1957, Toyota first came to the United States to market a small car called the Toyopet. The experiment was such a dismal failure that the company virtually withdrew from the US car market. They held on by selling a few off-road vehicles called Land Cruisers. Toyota studied the market carefully for several years, returning in full force in 1965 with the introduction of the Corona. They sold just 5,400 cars that year. Yet, not too many years later, Toyota was heralded as the largest importer of automobiles to the United States.

Most people toss in the towel if the public doesn't respond quickly to their products, service, or ideas. But those who operate by the principle of persistence are not so easily discouraged. They are like investors who purchase the same amount of stocks or mutual funds every month—no matter what the market is doing. These are the people who actually get excited when the prices of stocks are falling. They know that next month they will be buying many more shares with the same amount of money. When stock prices rise—and they always have—their assets skyrocket. Persistent investors who are in the market for the long run become wealthy in the process.

There are people everywhere who are sitting in the ashes of defeat, not knowing that dead ends are a part of the real world. The mere fact that you know something *didn't* work is a lesson in itself. You now know one more process you can eliminate on your journey to success.

What you need to understand about failure is that it doesn't happen until you abandon your plan. Setbacks will happen and should cause you to modify your strategy, while incorporating the lessons you learned.

George Bernard Shaw said, "When I was a young man, I observed that nine out of ten things I did were failures. I didn't want to be a failure so I did ten times more work."

When it comes to success, speed is not as important as steady progress. Turtles are never invited to participate in the Olympics, yet they reach their destinations. Perhaps we should look at their progress more closely. They have to stick their necks out to get anywhere.

Keeping Your Eye on the Goal

Will you make mistakes along the way? Count on it. Someone once said, "To err is human. It is only when the eraser wears out before the pencil that you know you're overdoing it."

When you know what you need to do, take immediate action and don't stop until you reach your goal. If you stub your toe, it's an indication that you weren't sitting down. You were actively involved. If you're not making any mistakes or experiencing any setbacks, chances are you're not doing anything.

Two men were once fishing about a mile from the shoreline when suddenly the boat began to leak. As the water poured in faster than they could bail it out, one of the men said, "Let's stop for a moment and pray for strength to swim all the way to shore."

His friend jumped in the water and said, "Come on. Let's pray while we're swimming."

Whether it is the shoreline or the highest mountain, once you have made that decision, don't take your eye off the goal. Jesus said, "No one having put his hand to the plow, and looking back, is fit for the kingdom of God" (Luke 9:62).

We all were born with a special gift of some kind. When you discover it, set a realistic plan to see that talent developed. Get out of your comfort zone and begin working on your objective with a consistent but driving passion.

Sailing On

If you know your goal is right, never, never yield. Remember, every successful person has a story about overcoming tremendous obstacles. Most have found that some of the greatest barriers are other people. It is imperative that you not allow anyone to intimidate you in the quest of your goal. When someone shows you the facts or gives you statistics that say you will fail, use the experience to strengthen your resolve to keep pressing forward.

The diary of Christopher Columbus seems at first to be quite repetitious.

"This day we sailed on." Storms were buffeting the ships.

"This day we sailed on." The *Pinto* was breaking apart.

"This day we sailed on." There was hunger and darkness. They sailed on! Why not make that your motto? Be determined to sail on when you know the decision you have made is correct.

Instead of looking around to see what the competition is doing, focus on your own progress. Never worry about those who are racing to reach great heights by any means possible. When they reach the top of the ladder, they may learn it's resting on the wrong building.

Be sure your climb is steady and deliberate, and make certain your foot touches every rung of the ladder. If you miss just one, you'll likely have to climb down and retrace your steps.

To help you reach your goal, ask one question on a daily basis: "What have I done to bring me closer to my objective?" Persistence pays.

celebrate a grand new you!

It's amazing what you have accomplished in just twenty-four hours.

If you are an adult of average weight, in one day your heart beats 103,689 times, you breathe 23,040 times, you inhale 438 cubic feet of air, you eat just over three pounds of food and drink almost three quarts of liquid. You speak 25,000 words and exercise seven million brain cells. That is quite a workout in just one day.

Now, you have been asked to add an even longer list of accomplishments. If you follow through on the commitments you've made during the hours you have spent with this book, your expanded list will include conscious accomplishments that only you could have achieved.

The great transformations of life are the result of deep and personal decisions. The fulfillment of your commitment may take weeks, months, or even years. But the change becomes reality because you took the time to decide.

The new you may not gain fame in a distant land. Your environment may stay the same, but you have become new. It begins right where you are. Russell Conwell, author of the classic inspirational book *Acres of Diamonds*, said, "He who would be great anywhere must be great in his own Philadelphia."

What about the Past?

As people change, they have a tendency to defend the past. When they focus on yesterday, however, they are only spinning their wheels. It's more important to focus on the new dream and use their energy to reach beyond themselves. The vision is empowering. The past is depleting.

Gerald Corey, professor of psychology at California State University at Fullerton, says,

> For so many people the power of the present is lost; instead of being in the present moment, they invest their energies in bemoaning their past mistakes and ruminating about how life could and should have been different, or they engage in endless resolutions and plans for the future. As they direct their energy toward what was or what might have been, their capacity to capitalize on the power of the present diminishes.

The moment you begin to rest on your laurels, you begin to live in the past. It is important to see yourself in the process of always changing, not as a finished product that is fixed in concrete.

Personalizing Conversation

The transformation you experience will find its expression in many areas, but it will be especially noticeable in your vocabulary. Words are a reflection of what is happening inside. You need to be aware of their power. By listening closely to what you are communicating, you can take greater control of your conversation. Here are some specifics.

Do your best to avoid "it" talk. For example, "It is difficult to start an exercise program," when you really mean, "I find it difficult . . ." When you use "it" instead of "I," you depersonalize your problem. Think of it this way: "Three 'it's' and you're out."

We can use "you" talk in the same manner. We say, "You feel disappointed when people don't say thanks." What we actually mean is, "I feel disappointed." We all need to personalize and own the problem in order to do something about it.

We also say, "I can't," when we really mean "I won't." When we say, "I can't," we feel powerless and out of control. Saying either "I will," or "I won't," shows that we have accepted personal responsibility. It keeps us in control, with a sense of power.

Now is also the time to bury the "shoulds" and the "oughts." If you think about those two words for a moment, you see how they foster guilt. If I say, "I should," I'm saying, "I don't really want to do this thing, but I think somebody wants me to." Say, "I choose to," or, "I want to." That produces a personal power of choice and helps your objective to become clear.

You need to be aware of the way you ask questions. Here's the rule to remember: Ask questions that begin with "what" and "how." Those questions get you somewhere. You begin to learn what you might do and how you might accomplish things. You garner needed information and knowledge from "what" and "how" questions.

When you begin with "why," you immediately place people on the defensive. Asking "Why did you do it that way?" implies criticism—"You should have done it differently." It also invites justification. And it puts you in the past, talking about why something happened the way it did, rather than about what you might now do to change it—and how you might proceed in the present. By asking questions like, "What is happening in your life now? What do you want to do? How do you feel about it?" of ourselves and others, you focus on the present.

Counselors encourage people to make personal statements that help them assume responsibility. *It*, *you*, and *why* statements are not personal. You can change your language to reflect your owner-ship of your life.

Inside Out

During these hours, we have emphasized the importance of changes that begin on the inside and work their way to the surface. After all, your character shines through in every action of your life. It is especially true when you are under pressure.

What you wear, what you say, and the expression on your face is a reflection of what you are.

At every step of your journey, continue to remind yourself that your identity does not need to be anchored in someone else's defi-nition of you. When you base who you are on what others say, you become a stranger to yourself.

How you feel about *you* is not based on doing, but on being. It's been said, "Being is happily achieving, while doing is achieving to be happy."

Many people link the term "growing pains" with children, but we will feel plenty of hurts and aches during the changes we make as adults. We are like fruit. Until it is ripe it continues to grow.

Take your cue from the mighty eagle. At the first sign of a storm, the eagle spreads its wings and climbs above the tempest. Adversity, in fact, allows it to use less effort. The eagle is designed to glide in the wind. The stronger the gale, the higher it can soar.

Turmoil also allows the eagle to fly faster. An eagle's normal speed is fifty miles per hour. In a storm, it can fly eighty or more miles per hour. But remember, the higher it flies, the more pressure it will encounter.

Some people, however, behave more like buzzards. They try to hide between the rocks and are harassed by those who would attack. They don't enjoy the storm; they just endure it.

You can become as an eagle and let difficulty work for you.

Time to Celebrate!

Life is a process of closing some doors and opening others—not a series of destinations but an exciting process. You can take joy in knowing that you have an eternal destiny that extends beyond time itself. It is this knowledge that can empower you on your journey.

During these twenty-four hours you have been challenged to make substantial changes in many areas of your life. Some theories of psychology are based on seeing the whole in order to understand the parts. We have concentrated on the parts in order to see the whole. Now you can stand back and see how the pieces of your puzzle come together.

What does it take for ultimate success?

If your family's for you, that will help!

If you were born into wealth, that will help!

If you have good credit, that will help!

If you are healthy, that will help!

Each of these factors may play a part, but there's only one key—*you*! That's what makes the difference.

The last chapters of your life have yet to be written. If you have made a resolution to change in only two or three areas, the growth process has begun. Remember that creativity helps you imagine how your transformation might take place. Visualizing what might be done and how it can be done gives you the courage and strength to make changes. It precedes action and enthusiasm which, in turn, engender new energy, the energy you will need to see the transformation to the end.

We ask that you reread this book one year from now to measure your progress. You are not comparing yourself to those around you, or even to the objectives on these pages. The real test is to see how far you have come from where you started. The following year, take the Turn-Around Test again. Do it until you have reached your goal in every area. Even then you'll still have room for your roots to grow deeper and your branches to spread wider.

In these twenty-four hours you may have grown one inch or one mile. Whatever your progress, take the time to celebrate a grand new you!

Notes

HOUR **2 Revalue Your Self-Worth**

1. James P. Comer, quoted in *Insight* 95 (1989): 39.
2. Erich Fromm, *The Art of Loving* (New York: Harper & Row, 1956), 50.
3. Maxwell Maltz, *Psycho-Cybernetics* (New York: Pocket Books, 1960), 6.

HOUR **3 A Transformed Thought-Life**

1. Albert E. Cliffe, *Lessons in Successful Living* (New York: Prentice-Hall, Inc., 1953), 19.
2. S. I. McMillen, *None of These Diseases* (Old Tappan, NJ: Fleming H. Revell Company, 1988), 116.
3. Edward De Bono, *New Think* (New York: Avon Books, 1971), 15.

HOUR **4 A New Look at Your Goals**

1. Bryan Tracy, *The Psychology of Achievement* (Chicago: Nightengale-Conant Corporation, cassette tape, 1986).
2. Charles F. Kettering, quoted in Joe Griffith, *Speaker's Library of Business Stories, Anecdotes, and Humor* (Englewood Cliffs, NJ: Prentice Hall, Inc., 1990), 129.
3. Ibid., adapted from p. 134.
4. Shad Helmstetter, *The Self-Talk Solution* (New York: Pocket Books, 1987), 141.

HOUR **5 Great Expectations**

1. Deborah Feltzer and C. A. Riessinger, *Journal of Sport and Exercise Psychology* (June 1990): 132–43.

HOUR 6 A Major Attitude Adjustment

1. Peter D. Ashworth, "Phenomenologically-based Empirical Studies of Social Attitude," *Journal of Phenomenological Psychology* 16 (1985): 69.

2. Viktor E. Frankl, *Man's Search for Meaning* (New York: Washington Square Press, 1968), 104.

HOUR 7 Choose Your New Team

1. Frederick S. Perls, *In and Out of the Garbage Pail* (New York: Bantam Books, 1969), 137, 147.

2. Warren E. Avis, *The Art of Sharing* (New York: Cornerstone Library Publications, 1974), 19.

HOUR 8 Bend without Breaking

1. Fred Bucy in Joe Griffith, *Speaker's Library*, 30.

2. Mark McCormack in Joe Griffith, *Speaker's Library*, 229.

HOUR 9 Say Farewell to Unhealthy Fear

1. M. Scott Peck, *The Road Less Traveled* (New York: Simon and Schuster, 1978), 17.

2. Susan Jeffers, *Feel the Fear and Do It Anyway* (New York: Fawcett Columbine, 1987), 22.

3. David Viscott, *Risking* (New York: Pocket Books, 1977), 20.

HOUR 10 Winning by Quitting

1. Horace Mann, quoted in Winston K. Pendleton, *Handbook of Inspiration and Motivational Stories* (West Nyack, NY: Parker Publishing Co., Inc., 1982), 131.

2. Jacquelyn Small, *The Therapist of the Future* (Marina del Ray, CA: DeVorss & Company, 1982), 69.

3. Lionel G. Standing and Bruce Nicholson, "Models for Student Drinking and Smoking: Parents or Peers?" *Social Behavior and Personality* 17 (1989): 223.

4. William H. Danforth, quoted in Charles B. Roth, *The Secrets of Success Encyclopedia* (New York: McGraw-Hill Book Co., 1965), 101.

5. Donald Laird and Eleanor Laird in Roth, *Secrets of Success*, 92.

HOUR 11 Take Charge of Your Emotions

1. David Viscott, *The Language of Feelings* (New York: Pocket Books, 1976), 150.

HOUR 12 Revolutionize Your Data Bank

1. Charles E. Jones, *Life Is Tremendous* (Wheaton, IL: Tyndale House, 1968), 73.
2. Jessamyn West in Joe Griffith, *Speaker's Library*, 194.
3. C. D. Board, quoted in Morton Kelsey, *Christianity as Psychology* (Minneapolis, MO: Augsburg Publishing House, 1986), 67.
4. Ken Lipke, personal interview, November 24, 1992.

HOUR 13 How to Reorder Your Day

1. Dale Carnegie in Joe Griffith, *Speaker's Library*, 356.
2. James A. Fields in Joe Griffith, *Speaker's Library*, 279.

HOUR 15 Your Newborn Body

1. Steven Locke and Douglas Colligan, *The Healer Within* (New York: Mentor Books, 1986), 7.

HOUR 16 The Look of a Winner

1. John T. Molloy, *Dress for Success* (New York: Warner Books, 1975), 25.

HOUR 17 The Discovery of Excellence

1. Les Giblin, *How to Have Confidence and Power in Dealing with People* (Englewood Cliffs, NJ: Prentice-Hall, Inc., 1956), 24.
2. Tom Peters, *A Passion for Excellence* (New York: Random House, 1985), 20.

HOUR 18 A Brand-New Heart

1. Redford Williams, *The Trusting Heart* (New York: Times Books, 1989), 71.

HOUR 19 From Master to Servant

1. Larry Scherwitz, quoted in Emrika Padus, *Your Emotions and Your Health* (Emmaus, Pa.: Rodale Press, Inc., 1986), 122.
2. Fromm, *The Art of Loving*, 19.
3. Dale Carnegie, *How to Win Friends and Influence People* (New York: Pocket Books, 1936), 55.

HOUR 20 A Lifestyle of Laughter

1. Bernie S. Siegel, *Love, Medicine, and Miracles* (New York: Caedmon, cassette tape, 1988).

HOUR **21 Up with Enthusiasm!**

1. Vince Lombardi in Joe Griffith, *Speaker's Library*, 104.

HOUR **22 Your Key to Daily Renewal**

1. Elbert Hubbard, "A Message to Garcia," in *The Compact Treasury of Inspiration* (New York: Pillar Books, 1977), 31.

Jim Hartness, trained in psychotherapy at the University of North Carolina graduate school, is a pastor, counselor, and seminar and conference speaker. He is the author of *Escape: Freedom from Life's Greatest Traps*.

Neil Eskelin is a distinguished motivational speaker and author. His books include *Yes Yes Living in a No No World, What to Do When You Don't Know What to Do,* and *101 Promises Worth Keeping*.

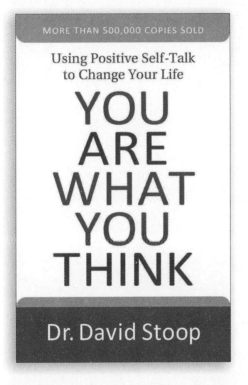

FIND FREEDOM IN THE
Gifts of Work and Rest

In this burden-lifting book, Glynnis Whitwer helps you examine your heart and your schedule in order to seek a healthy, holy, and enjoyable balance between work and rest. She shows you how to prioritize your goals and your time, how to be present in the moment as Jesus was, and how to find the freedom of true soul rest.